GUIDELINES
PESACH HAGGADAH
הגדה של פסח

The GUIDELINES
PESACH HAGGADAH

הַגָּדָה שֶׁל פֶּסַח

First published 2013
Second revised edition published 2015, 2026
Copyright © 2013, 2015, 2026 by E. Barclay & Y. Jaeger
ISBN 9781614654957

All rights reserved
No part of this publication may be translated, reproduced, stored in a retrieval system, or
transmitted in any form or by any means, electronic, mechanical, photocopying, recording, or
otherwise, without prior permission in writing from the copyright holders and the publisher.

**Please address any questions or comments
regarding the GUIDELINES books to the authors:**
E. Barclay (02) 583 0914
Y. Jaeger (02) 583 4889
email: 5834889@gmail.com

Volumes in the GUIDELINES series:

Candle Lighting & Separating Challah	*Preparing Food on Shabbos*	*The Magnificent Months*
The Simcha Handbook	*Kiddush & Havdalah*	*Tefillah*
Mourning	*Yom Tov & Chol Hamoed*	*Brachos*
Family Purity	*Bishul*	*Yichud*
Honoring Parents	*Borer*	*Shemittah*
Tevilas Keilim	*Muktzeh*	*Shaatnez*

Published by:
Menucha Publishers Inc.
250 44th Street Suite #B2 Brooklyn N.Y. 11232
Tel/Fax: 718-232-0856
1-855-menucha

sales@menuchapublishers.com
www.menuchapublishers.com

The
Guidelines
PESACH HAGGADAH

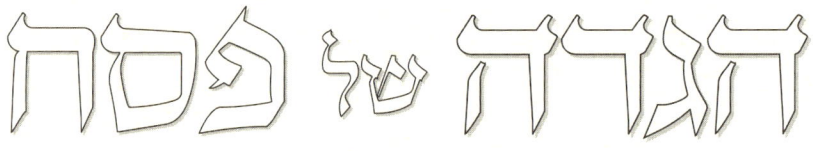

A Complete Step-by-Step Guide to
the Laws of the Seder
with a New Lucid Translation
of the Haggadah

Rabbi Elozor Barclay
Rabbi Yitzchok Jaeger

MENUCHA
PUBLISHERS

A Menucha Press Book

(Translation of Hebrew Original)

Rabbi CHAIM P. SCHEINBERG
Rosh Hayeshiva "TORAH ORE"
and Morah Hora'ah of Kiryat Mattersdorf

הרב חיים פינחס שיינברג

ראש ישיבת "תורה אור"
ומורה הוראה דקרית מטרסדורף

בס"ד, חודש שבט, תשס"ג

מכתב ברכה

I was pleased to see "**Guidelines**", an impressive six volume work which encompasses the *halachos* of the *Moadim* and other relevant topics, written by Rabbi Elozor Barclay, *shlita* and Rabbi Yitzchok Jaeger, *shlita*. These books have been praised highly by numerous *Gedolei HaRabbonim* and have been received warmly by the English speaking Torah community.

As a matter of policy, I do not endorse *halachic* rulings in any published *sefer*. However, since so many *Gedolei Torah* have already agreed to what is written and offered their approbation to "**Guidelines**", I join them and offer my heartfelt blessing that *Hashem* should guide and assist the authors in producing more successful *halachic* works, which glorify and strengthen the Torah.

Signed in the honor of the Torah,

Rabbi Chaim Pinchas Scheinberg

רחוב פנים מאירות 2, ירושלים, ת.ד. 6979, טל. 1513-537 (02), ישראל
2 Panim Meirot St., Jerusalem, P.O.B. 6979, Tel. (02) 537-1513, Israel

RABBI ZEV LEFF
Rabbi of Moshav Matisyahu
Rosh Hayeshiva Yeshiva Gedola Matisyahu

בס״ד

ט״ז שבט תשס״ג

It is with great pleasure that I reviewed the manuscript of "**Guidelines**" to Pesach by Rabbi Elozor Barclay שליט״א and Rabbi Yitzchok Jaeger שליט״א.

A siyum – completion – is a very special and joyous occasion. This volume is a siyum and culminates the series of **Guidelines** to the various Yomim Tovim of the year. As in the previous volumes, the laws and customs are presented in a concise, lucid, and organized fashion. The fact that the vastness of the laws of Pesach could be condensed so masterfully into this volume of **Guidelines** is truly impressive. This volume, as well as the entire complete series of Guidelines, will serve as a guide for those who cannot learn these laws from their original sources, and as a valuable aid even to those who can.

May Hashem grant the authors the ability to continue to benefit Klal Yisrael with further works of Torah and mitzvos for many long happy and healthy years.

With Torah blessings,

Rabbi Zev Leff

May the learning of this sefer be לעילוי נשמת
and a זכות for the נשמות of our dear parents

ר' יצחק ב"ר גדליה ז"ל
מרת אסתר בת ר' פישל הכהן ע"ה
ר' אליעזר ב"ר ראובן הלוי ז"ל
מרת שפרה רבקה בת ר' מאיר יוסף ע"ה

ת.נ.צ.ב.ה.

Dedicated by Judith and Ira Weiss

לע"נ

ר' יוסף שמואל ב"ר אלעזר ז"ל
מרת חנה רחל בת ר' יצחק אריה הכהן ע"ה

Dedicated in memory of our
beloved parents
**Samuel Joseph and Anne Rachela
Barclay**

ת.נ.צ.ב.ה.

לע"נ

ר' ישראל ב"ר מאיר טרעפ ז"ל
נפטר כ"ד טבת תשע"ה

ואשתו

מרת פיגא העניא בת ר' עובדיה הלוי ע"ה
נפטרה כ"ד סיון תשס"ו

ת.נ.צ.ב.ה.

Table of Contents

Foreword		9
Chapter One:	*Bedikas Chametz*	11
Chapter Two:	Fast of the First-born	17
Chapter Three:	Erev Pesach	19
Chapter Four:	*Eiruv Tavshilin*	29
Chapter Five:	Candle Lighting	33
Chapter Six:	Preparations for the Seder	37
Chapter Seven:	When Pesach falls on Sunday	47
Chapter Eight:	The Seder	50
Glossary		151
Hebrew Sources		153

Foreword

With praise and thanks to Hashem, we present to the public the Guidelines edition of the Pesach Haggadah. When the Guidelines series was launched over ten years ago, the first publication was a booklet of Questions and Answers about the laws of Pesach. This was soon reproduced as "Guidelines to Pesach" which addresses more than five hundred of the most commonly asked questions about Pesach and includes all the detailed laws of the Seder.

Since then, Hashem has granted us the merit to produce works covering a large range of topics all of which are presented in the popular style of Questions and Answers. For the first time we have deviated from this style in order to create a lucid, practical, *halacha* oriented Haggadah. The general laws of *erev Pesach* are presented first in clear detail from *Bedikas Chametz* until the final preparations for the Seder. This is followed by the text of the Haggadah, interspersed with

step-by-step instructions at every appropriate place. This form of presentation will enable the reader to conduct the Seder with confidence and fulfill all the mitzvos correctly to the last detail. In addition, we have provided a new clear translation of the entire text for those who are not so familiar with the Hebrew language. This has been placed conveniently alongside the text making it immediately accessible when required. Especially noteworthy is the translation of the songs at the conclusion of the Haggadah. Even scholars will appreciate the great effort that has been invested to bring clarity to their esoteric words and phrases.

Rarely will a written work be a perfect substitute for a one-to-one discussion with a rav. The answer to a query often depends upon various factors that only further questioning can clarify. Even though much thought and effort has been invested in the phrasing and wording used, it is possible that halachos may be misunderstood or misconstrued. Our primary intent is to guide the reader through these laws, hence the title Guidelines.

We would like to express our thanks to Rav Yirmiyahu Kaganoff, *shlita*, posek in Neveh Ya'akov, who with his keen perception and comprehensive mastery of the topics, provided many valuable changes and additions throughout the entire book. Many thanks also to Reb Yerachmiel Goldberg and Reb Pinchas Goldstein for checking the text meticulously.

We would like to express our appreciation for the devoted work of Reb Shmuel Kaffe who has been designing outstanding covers for the entire Guidelines series for over a decade. Thanks also go to Mrs. Feige Savitsky for her expertise in designing the entire layout of this Haggadah.

It is our hope that in the merit of fulfilling the mitzvos of the Seder punctiliously, Hashem will perform miracles and wonders for us and redeem us from exile, as He did for our ancestors in the days of old.

Elozor Barclay   Yitzchok Jaeger

Yerushalayim, Shevat 5773

Chapter One

Bedikas Chametz

1. *Bedikas Chametz* should be done at nightfall on the evening of the fourteenth of Nissan.

2. If a person is unable to begin the search at nightfall, he should begin as soon as possible.

3. The custom is to *daven Ma'ariv* at nightfall and do *Bedikas Chametz* immediately afterwards.

4. A person who intends to *daven Ma'ariv* later in the evening or missed the minyan at nightfall should do *Bedikas Chametz* immediately at nightfall. According to some opinions, he should delay searching for chametz until after *davening Ma'ariv*. One should make an effort to *daven Ma'ariv* immediately at nightfall in order to avoid this situation.

5. A person who is usually at work at nightfall must make every effort to start *Bedikas Chametz* at nightfall. Therefore, he should leave his place of work early in order to do *Bedikas Chametz* on time.

6. Ideally, one's office should be searched on the night of the fourteenth of Nissan. If it is far from the house and it is inconvenient to travel there on the night of the fourteenth, he should include the office in the sale of chametz (provided he will not be there during *Chol Hamoed*). Alternatively, he should search the office without a *b'racha* on the last evening possible (see also no. 7).

7. If a person or a family leaves the house before the night of the fourteenth, one must perform *Bedikas Chametz* on the evening before departure, unless he sells the entire house (see no. 9). In this situation, all the rules of *Bedikas Chametz* apply (e.g. searching at nightfall, not working or eating beforehand), except that a *b'racha* is not recited, and it is not necessary to

distribute ten pieces of bread. The nullification should be said as usual after the search.

8. A visitor is not required to do *Bedikas Chametz* even if he is given a private room in the host's house or a vacant house. This includes married children who go to their parents for Pesach.

9. A visitor is required to do *Bedikas Chametz* at his own home on the night of the fourteenth. If he goes to his host before the night of the fourteenth, he should do *Bedikas Chametz* without a *b'racha* on the night before he leaves home. If he is selling the entire house to a gentile, he is exempt from *Bedikas Chametz* (see no. 24). According to some opinions, one part of the house should not be sold, so that he can fulfill the mitzvah of *Bedikas Chametz* there.

10. If a visitor pays rent, the visitor is obligated to do *Bedikas Chametz* there.

11. If this is only a 'token' arrangement in order to artificially create an obligation to do *Bedikas Chametz*, opinions differ whether it is effective. If such an arrangement is made, the visitor should do *Bedikas Chametz* in his room, but he should listen to the *b'racha* being recited by the homeowner rather than recite it himself.

12. Students who live in a yeshiva or seminary are obligated to do *Bedikas Chametz* in their rooms on the night of the fourteenth with a *b'racha*. If they intend to leave the yeshiva or seminary before the night of the fourteenth, they should do *Bedikas Chametz* without a *b'racha* on the evening before they leave (see no. 9). Alternatively, they may appoint someone else to do the search for them on the night of the fourteenth.

13. One must not start any new activity within half-an-hour before nightfall. This includes having a haircut, shaving, and bathing. When a person is involved in various activities he might not notice the passage of time, and he might miss the ideal time to do *Bedikas Chametz*. If one began before the half-hour period, one may continue until nightfall. At nightfall, one must stop all activities.

14. According to some opinions, it is forbidden to begin studying Torah at home during this half-hour. If one appoints another person to remind him to do *Bedikas Chametz* on time, he is permitted to study. It is permitted to study Torah in shul while waiting for *Ma'ariv*.

15. During the half-hour before nightfall, one

may not eat more than a *kebeitza* of bread or cake. There is no restriction on other foods or drinks during this period. At nightfall, one should begin the search without delay (or *daven Ma'ariv*).

16. It is forbidden to go to sleep within the half-hour before nightfall since there is a strong possibility that one may oversleep.

17. These restrictions only apply to a person who has to do *Bedikas Chametz*. Therefore, the wife and children of a married man are not restricted. However, a woman who lives alone or whose husband is away must keep all the above restrictions since she must do *Bedikas Chametz*.

18. In order that the search can be performed with a *b'racha* in a house that is completely clean, the custom is to distribute ten pieces of bread around the house before the search. Whoever puts out the pieces should make a note of where they are located in case any are not found during the search.

19. Each of these pieces should be less than the size of a *kezayis*. The pieces should be wrapped well to ensure that they do not leave crumbs behind.

20. If one did not find all the pieces during the search, he should make every effort to find them. If they are still not found, one may rely on the declaration that all unseen chametz shall be null and void.

21. When doing *Bedikas Chametz*, one must check very thoroughly for chametz, and it is not sufficient to simply look for the ten pieces of bread. All parts of the house where chametz might have been brought during the year must be checked that they are now free of chametz. This is done by confirming that such areas have indeed been thoroughly cleaned and that no chametz has subsequently been brought there (see check-list in no. 39). Before the search, one should put out of children's reach all chametz that is to be sold to a gentile or that one wishes to eat. Similarly, all chametz found during the search should be put in a safe place until it is burned the next morning.

22. One must check any area where chametz may have been brought during the year. Since it is common for small children to carry food around the house, one must check any area that they may have entered.

23. The main custom is not to search the areas that are being sold to a gentile since any chametz there will in any case be sold. One may even deliberately avoid checking sections of the house for chametz and include them in the sale. A person who does not wish to rely on the sale for food items that are unquestionably chametz should search these areas for such items.

24. Ideally, one should follow the traditional custom to conduct the search with a wax candle rather than use a flashlight.

25. In places where a person is hesitant to take a candle (e.g. a linen closet), a flashlight must be used.

26. The electric lights may be left on if this facilitates the search. If they disturb the effectiveness of the candle or flashlight, they should be turned off.

27. If a person forgot to recite the *b'racha*, he should still recite it if the search has not yet been concluded.

28. If a person finished the entire search without reciting the *b'racha*, according to many opinions he may recite it just before he burns the chametz on the following day.

29. Ideally, the homeowner himself should do the search. If he wishes, he may ask another person to assist in the search. In extenuating circumstances, he may even ask another person to do the entire search on his behalf.

30. If the other people are going to assist in the search, they should listen to the *b'racha* that the homeowner recites and say 'amen'.

31. If the homeowner himself is unable to participate in the search, the person who is doing the search should recite the *b'racha*. If possible, the homeowner himself should recite the *b'racha* and search a little.

32. It is forbidden to speak after reciting the *b'racha* before beginning the search. A person who spoke must repeat the *b'racha* unless what he said was connected to the search.

33. If he spoke during the search, the *b'racha* should not be repeated even if he spoke about unrelated matters. However, in order not to be distracted from the search, one should not speak unnecessarily until after he has said the nullification. Similarly, telephone calls should not be made or answered unless this concerns the search.

34. A person should not repeat the *b'racha* if he has more than one property to search, but he should go without interruption from one place to the other and continue his search there.

35. If he was unavoidably interrupted between checking two properties, he should not repeat the *b'racha*.

36. If a person forgot to nullify the chametz immediately after the search, he should say the nullification as soon as he remembers.

37. Some have the custom to say the nullification three times.

38. The following is a suggested list of items and places where chametz might be found, some of which might be easily overlooked: arts and crafts supplies (might contain noodles, barley etc.), baby carriage, baking utensils, basement, *benschers*, bird cage, bird food, briefcase, car (especially glove compartment and trunk), cook books, crib, fish food, garbage cans, handbags, high chair, knapsack, medicine box, office, pet food, playpen, porch, school bags, shopping bags, storage room, stroller, suitcases, tallis bag, toy box, *zemiros* books.

Before beginning the search one should recite the following b'racha.
Before reciting this b'racha, a person should have in mind that he is starting to fulfill the mitzvah to destroy his chametz and will conclude the mitzvah when he burns it.

Blessed are You, Hashem our God, King of the universe, Who has sanctified us with His commandments and commanded us to destroy chametz.

בָּרוּךְ אַתָּה יְיָ אֱלֹהֵינוּ מֶלֶךְ הָעוֹלָם,
אֲשֶׁר קִדְּשָׁנוּ בְּמִצְוֹתָיו, וְצִוָּנוּ עַל
בְּעוּר חָמֵץ:

The Guidelines Haggadah

> **The first nullification of chametz should be said immediately after the search.**
> **If a person does not understand the Aramaic words, he should say the declaration in English.**

All chametz and leaven that is in my possession that I have not seen, that I have not destroyed, and that I do not know about, shall be null and ownerless like the dust of the earth.

כָּל חֲמִירָא וַחֲמִיעָא דְּאִכָּא בִרְשׁוּתִי, דְּלָא חֲמִתֵּהּ, וּדְלָא בִעַרְתֵּהּ, וּדְלָא יְדַעְנָא לֵיהּ, לִבָּטֵל וְלֶהֱוֵי הֶפְקֵר כְּעַפְרָא דְאַרְעָא:

Chapter Two

Fast of the First-born

39. First-borns are required to fast on *erev Pesach*. If *erev Pesach* is on Shabbos, the fast is on the previous Thursday.

40. The fast begins at *halachic* dawn. Although the custom is to attend a *Siyum* in shul, one must be careful not to have a drink at home before *Shacharis*.

41. The first-born son of either the father or the mother is required to fast. The custom is that first-born girls do not fast. A first-born son following a miscarriage (*chas veshalom*) is required to fast, as is a first-born son of a *cohen* or a *levi*.

42. Since there is a doubt whether a first-born convert is required to fast, it is recommended that he attend a *Siyum* with the other first-borns. If he is unable to attend a *Siyum*, he does not have to fast.

43. The same applies to a boy born by Cesarean section.

44. A boy below bar mitzvah is not required to fast, but the father should fast in his place. This applies to a first-born son between the ages of thirty days and bar mitzvah. If the father is himself a first-born, the fast is valid for both himself and his son.

45. It has become the accepted custom for a first-born to attend a *Siyum* and partake of the refreshments served. Similarly, he is permitted

to join a *Seudas Mitzvah*, such as a *Bris* or *Pidyon Haben*. After this, he may eat throughout the day.

46.   Ideally, the first-borns should listen to the conclusion of the volume studied. If they listened but did not understand, or if they missed the conclusion, they may nevertheless partake of the refreshments.

47.   If possible, one should eat enough to recite a *B'racha Acharona*.

48.   If a first-born heard the *Siyum*, he may break his fast at home, although ideally he should try to eat some of the refreshments provided at the *Siyum*.

49.   A *Siyum* may be made on completion of any one of the following: a tractate of Talmud Bavli or Talmud Yerushalmi, one of the six orders of the Mishnah, one of the books of *Nach* studied in depth, one of the four volumes of the *Shulchan Aruch*.

50.   One may deliberately hurry or delay the completion of a volume in order to make a *Siyum* on *erev Pesach*.

51.   A mourner may participate in a *Siyum*. However, if he is in the week of shiva he may not go to shul, but he should arrange for someone to come to his house to make a *Siyum*.

52.   First-borns may participate in a *Siyum* made by a boy below bar mitzvah as long as the boy studied the volume seriously and understood it to the best of his ability.

53.   If a first-born is unable to attend a *Siyum*, he should try to fast all day. If he has a headache or doesn't feel well, he may break the fast. Similarly, if fasting will prevent him from properly fulfilling the mitzvos of the Seder night, he need not fast. In either case, he should limit himself to just a small amount of food.

54.   One may make or attend a *Siyum* before *Shacharis*, but he must not eat the refreshments until after *Shacharis*.

Chapter Three

Erev Pesach

55. On *erev Pesach*, one should *daven Shacharis* early in order to finish eating and burning the chametz by the required time.

56. Chametz may be eaten until the end of the fourth *halachic* hour of the day. The exact time should be found in the local Jewish calendar.

57. After one has finished eating chametz, he should clean his teeth thoroughly.

58. The remaining chametz should be destroyed together with the ten pieces of bread that were collected during *Bedikas Chametz*. The custom is to destroy it by burning, but if this is too difficult, one should first throw the majority of the chametz into a public garbage container, and leave at least a *kezayis* to be burned.

59. Paraffin should not be poured onto the chametz in the fire unless one is concerned that it would not otherwise be burned thoroughly. Edible oils may be poured onto the chametz to increase the fire.

60. One should remember to empty the domestic garbage bins and vacuum cleaner bags.

61. Some people have the custom to throw their old *lulav* into the fire.

62. It is not sufficient for the pieces of chametz to be blackened on the outside since the inside may still be edible. One must therefore remain by the fire to ensure that the chametz is thoroughly burned. If attempts to burn the chametz are failing, one should destroy it by any method or throw it into a public garbage container.

63. All the chametz must be burned or destroyed before the end of the fifth *halachic* hour of the day. The exact time should be found in the local Jewish calendar.

The Guidelines Haggadah

64.   If a person cannot make a fire, the chametz should be disposed of in another way, e.g. by throwing it into a public garbage container or flushing it down the toilet.

65.   One should also make a final check in one's pockets to ensure that no crumbs are there.

66.   The nullification that is made at night does not include chametz that is deliberately left or will be bought on the following day. The nullification that is made in the morning includes any remaining chametz that has not been destroyed. It also includes the chametz that is sold to the gentile in the event that something invalidates the sale.

67.   The daytime nullification must be said before the deadline for burning chametz.

68.   The morning nullification should be said by everyone who is over the age of bar or bas mitzvah (including married women). This is in case he (or she) owns personal items containing chametz.

After the chametz has been completely destroyed, one should say the final nullification. If he does not understand the Aramaic words, he should say the declaration in English.

All chametz and leaven that is in my possession that I have seen and that I have not seen, that I have destroyed and that I have not destroyed, shall be null and ownerless like the dust of the earth.

כָּל חֲמִירָא וַחֲמִיעָא דְּאִכָּא בִרְשׁוּתִי, דַּחֲזִתֵּהּ וּדְלָא חֲזִתֵּהּ, דַּחֲמִתֵּהּ וּדְלָא חֲמִתֵּהּ, דְּבִעַרְתֵּהּ וּדְלָא בִעַרְתֵּהּ, לִבָּטֵל וְלֶהֱוֵי הֶפְקֵר כְּעַפְרָא דְּאַרְעָא:

69. From *halachic* midday one may generally not do any type of work that is forbidden on *Chol Hamoed*.

70. It is permitted to have a haircut or shave before *halachic* midday, but after that it is permitted only when done by a gentile.

71. It is permitted to cut one's nails all day, but one should preferably do so before *halachic* midday.

72. Laundering is forbidden after *halachic* midday. If the washing machine started before that time, it may be left to finish the wash.

73. Clothes may be put into the dryer all day.

74. Clothes that are needed for Pesach may be ironed all day.

75. Shoes may be polished all day.

76. It is permitted to make repairs to a garment all day, but it is forbidden to complete the finishing touches to a new garment after *halachic* midday.

77. It is forbidden to eat matza all day.

78. The main custom is not to eat not matza on the evening of *erev Pesach*.

79. Children who are old enough to understand the story of *Yetzias Mitzrayim* should not eat matza.

80. According to most opinions, baked foods containing matza meal are also forbidden.

81. Those who eat *gebroktz* may eat boiled or fried foods containing matza meal (e.g. kneidlach), but only until the beginning of the tenth *halachic* hour (halfway between *halachic* noon and sunset).

82. The custom is not to eat *kitniyos* from the time that chametz may not be eaten. In times

The Guidelines Haggadah

of need, one may be lenient all day if the food has a reliable hechsher for Pesach.

83. Foods such as meat, fish, eggs, fruit, and vegetables may be eaten all day. However, from the beginning of the tenth *halachic* hour one should eat with moderation in order to eat the matza in the evening with appetite.

84. It is correct to *daven Mincha* early (*Mincha Gedola*) since in the *Beis Hamikdash* the afternoon sacrifice was brought earlier than usual to allow time for the *Korban Pesach*.

85. Following *Mincha*, many people have the custom to recite *Seder Korban Pesach*, which is a collection of verses from *Tanach* describing the bringing of the *Korban Pesach*. We pray that this recital be considered as if we have actually brought the *Korban Pesach*.

86. In the days of the *Beis Hamikdash*, men were obligated to purify themselves in a *mikveh* before every Yom Tov. Today, it is not an obligation but a widespread custom. Even if a man does not immerse on *erev Shabbos*, he should make an effort to do so on *erev Yom Tov*.

87. The correct time to go to the *mikveh* is after *halachic* midday.

Seder Korban Pesach

רִבּוֹן הָעוֹלָמִים, אַתָּה צִוִּיתָנוּ לְהַקְרִיב קָרְבַּן הַפֶּסַח בְּמוֹעֲדוֹ בְּאַרְבָּעָה עָשָׂר יוֹם לַחֹדֶשׁ הָרִאשׁוֹן, וְלִהְיוֹת כֹּהֲנִים בַּעֲבוֹדָתָם וּלְוִיִּם בְּדוּכָנָם וְיִשְׂרָאֵל בְּמַעֲמָדָם קוֹרְאִים אֶת הַהַלֵּל. וְעַתָּה בַּעֲוֹנוֹתֵינוּ חָרַב בֵּית הַמִּקְדָּשׁ וּבָטֵל קָרְבַּן הַפֶּסַח, וְאֵין לָנוּ לֹא כֹהֵן בַּעֲבוֹדָתוֹ וְלֹא לֵוִי בְּדוּכָנוֹ וְלֹא יִשְׂרָאֵל בְּמַעֲמָדוֹ, וְלֹא נוּכַל לְהַקְרִיב הַיּוֹם קָרְבַּן פֶּסַח. אֲבָל אַתָּה אָמַרְתָּ וּנְשַׁלְּמָה פָרִים שְׂפָתֵינוּ. לָכֵן יְהִי רָצוֹן מִלְּפָנֶיךָ יְיָ אֱלֹהֵינוּ וֵאלֹהֵי אֲבוֹתֵינוּ שֶׁיִּהְיֶה שִׂיחַ שִׂפְתוֹתֵינוּ חָשׁוּב לְפָנֶיךָ כְּאִלּוּ הִקְרַבְנוּ אֶת הַפֶּסַח בְּמוֹעֲדוֹ וְעָמַדְנוּ עַל מַעֲמָדוֹ, וְדִבְּרוּ הַלְוִיִּם בְּשִׁיר וְהַלֵּל לְהוֹדוֹת לַיְיָ. וְאַתָּה תְּכוֹנֵן מִקְדָּשְׁךָ עַל מְכוֹנוֹ, וְנַעֲשֶׂה וְנַקְרִיב לְפָנֶיךָ אֶת הַפֶּסַח בְּמוֹעֲדוֹ, כְּמוֹ שֶׁכָּתַבְתָּ עָלֵינוּ בְּתוֹרָתֶךָ עַל יְדֵי מֹשֶׁה עַבְדֶּךָ כָּאָמוּר:

שמות יב:א-יא

וַיֹּאמֶר יְהֹוָה אֶל מֹשֶׁה וְאֶל אַהֲרֹן בְּאֶרֶץ מִצְרַיִם לֵאמֹר: הַחֹדֶשׁ הַזֶּה לָכֶם רֹאשׁ חֳדָשִׁים רִאשׁוֹן הוּא לָכֶם לְחָדְשֵׁי הַשָּׁנָה: דַּבְּרוּ אֶל כָּל עֲדַת יִשְׂרָאֵל לֵאמֹר בֶּעָשֹׂר לַחֹדֶשׁ הַזֶּה וְיִקְחוּ לָהֶם אִישׁ שֶׂה לְבֵית אָבֹת שֶׂה לַבָּיִת: וְאִם יִמְעַט הַבַּיִת מִהְיֹת מִשֶּׂה וְלָקַח הוּא וּשְׁכֵנוֹ הַקָּרֹב אֶל בֵּיתוֹ בְּמִכְסַת נְפָשֹׁת אִישׁ לְפִי אָכְלוֹ תָּכֹסּוּ עַל הַשֶּׂה: שֶׂה תָמִים זָכָר בֶּן שָׁנָה יִהְיֶה לָכֶם מִן הַכְּבָשִׂים וּמִן הָעִזִּים תִּקָּחוּ: וְהָיָה לָכֶם לְמִשְׁמֶרֶת עַד אַרְבָּעָה עָשָׂר יוֹם לַחֹדֶשׁ הַזֶּה וְשָׁחֲטוּ אֹתוֹ כֹּל קְהַל עֲדַת יִשְׂרָאֵל בֵּין הָעַרְבָּיִם: וְלָקְחוּ מִן הַדָּם וְנָתְנוּ עַל שְׁתֵּי הַמְּזוּזֹת וְעַל הַמַּשְׁקוֹף עַל הַבָּתִּים אֲשֶׁר יֹאכְלוּ אֹתוֹ בָּהֶם: וְאָכְלוּ אֶת הַבָּשָׂר בַּלַּיְלָה הַזֶּה צְלִי אֵשׁ וּמַצּוֹת עַל מְרֹרִים יֹאכְלֻהוּ: אַל תֹּאכְלוּ מִמֶּנּוּ נָא וּבָשֵׁל מְבֻשָּׁל

בַּמַּיִם כִּי אִם צְלִי אֵשׁ רֹאשׁוֹ עַל כְּרָעָיו וְעַל קִרְבּוֹ: וְלֹא תוֹתִירוּ מִמֶּנּוּ עַד בֹּקֶר וְהַנֹּתָר מִמֶּנּוּ עַד בֹּקֶר בָּאֵשׁ תִּשְׂרֹפוּ: וְכָכָה תֹּאכְלוּ אֹתוֹ מָתְנֵיכֶם חֲגֻרִים נַעֲלֵיכֶם בְּרַגְלֵיכֶם וּמַקֶּלְכֶם בְּיֶדְכֶם וַאֲכַלְתֶּם אֹתוֹ בְּחִפָּזוֹן פֶּסַח הוּא לַיהֹוָה:

שמות יב:כא-כח

וַיִּקְרָא מֹשֶׁה לְכָל זִקְנֵי יִשְׂרָאֵל וַיֹּאמֶר אֲלֵהֶם מִשְׁכוּ וּקְחוּ לָכֶם צֹאן לְמִשְׁפְּחֹתֵיכֶם וְשַׁחֲטוּ הַפָּסַח: וּלְקַחְתֶּם אֲגֻדַּת אֵזוֹב וּטְבַלְתֶּם בַּדָּם אֲשֶׁר בַּסַּף וְהִגַּעְתֶּם אֶל הַמַּשְׁקוֹף וְאֶל שְׁתֵּי הַמְּזוּזֹת מִן הַדָּם אֲשֶׁר בַּסָּף וְאַתֶּם לֹא תֵצְאוּ אִישׁ מִפֶּתַח בֵּיתוֹ עַד בֹּקֶר: וְעָבַר יְהֹוָה לִנְגֹּף אֶת מִצְרַיִם וְרָאָה אֶת הַדָּם עַל הַמַּשְׁקוֹף וְעַל שְׁתֵּי הַמְּזוּזֹת וּפָסַח יְהֹוָה עַל הַפֶּתַח וְלֹא יִתֵּן הַמַּשְׁחִית לָבֹא אֶל בָּתֵּיכֶם לִנְגֹּף: וּשְׁמַרְתֶּם אֶת הַדָּבָר הַזֶּה לְחָק לְךָ וּלְבָנֶיךָ עַד עוֹלָם: וְהָיָה כִּי תָבֹאוּ אֶל הָאָרֶץ אֲשֶׁר יִתֵּן יְהֹוָה לָכֶם כַּאֲשֶׁר דִּבֵּר וּשְׁמַרְתֶּם אֶת הָעֲבֹדָה הַזֹּאת: וְהָיָה כִּי יֹאמְרוּ אֲלֵיכֶם בְּנֵיכֶם מָה הָעֲבֹדָה הַזֹּאת לָכֶם: וַאֲמַרְתֶּם זֶבַח פֶּסַח הוּא לַיהֹוָה אֲשֶׁר

פֶּסַח עַל בָּתֵּי בְנֵי יִשְׂרָאֵל בְּמִצְרַיִם בְּנָגְפּוֹ אֶת מִצְרַיִם וְאֶת בָּתֵּינוּ הִצִּיל וַיִּקֹּד הָעָם וַיִּשְׁתַּחֲווּ: וַיֵּלְכוּ וַיַּעֲשׂוּ בְּנֵי יִשְׂרָאֵל כַּאֲשֶׁר צִוָּה יְהֹוָה אֶת מֹשֶׁה וְאַהֲרֹן כֵּן עָשׂוּ:

שמות יב:מג-נ

וַיֹּאמֶר יְהֹוָה אֶל מֹשֶׁה וְאַהֲרֹן זֹאת חֻקַּת הַפָּסַח כָּל בֶּן נֵכָר לֹא יֹאכַל בּוֹ: וְכָל עֶבֶד אִישׁ מִקְנַת כָּסֶף וּמַלְתָּה אֹתוֹ אָז יֹאכַל בּוֹ: תּוֹשָׁב וְשָׂכִיר לֹא יֹאכַל בּוֹ: בְּבַיִת אֶחָד יֵאָכֵל לֹא תוֹצִיא מִן הַבַּיִת מִן הַבָּשָׂר חוּצָה וְעֶצֶם לֹא תִשְׁבְּרוּ בוֹ: כָּל עֲדַת יִשְׂרָאֵל יַעֲשׂוּ אֹתוֹ: וְכִי יָגוּר אִתְּךָ גֵּר וְעָשָׂה פֶסַח לַיהֹוָה הִמּוֹל לוֹ כָל זָכָר וְאָז יִקְרַב לַעֲשֹׂתוֹ וְהָיָה כְּאֶזְרַח הָאָרֶץ וְכָל עָרֵל לֹא יֹאכַל בּוֹ: תּוֹרָה אַחַת יִהְיֶה לָאֶזְרָח וְלַגֵּר הַגָּר בְּתוֹכְכֶם: וַיַּעֲשׂוּ כָּל בְּנֵי יִשְׂרָאֵל כַּאֲשֶׁר צִוָּה יְהֹוָה אֶת מֹשֶׁה וְאֶת אַהֲרֹן כֵּן עָשׂוּ:

ויקרא כג:ד-ה

אֵלֶּה מוֹעֲדֵי יְהֹוָה מִקְרָאֵי קֹדֶשׁ אֲשֶׁר תִּקְרְאוּ

אַתֶּם בְּמוֹעֲדָם: בַּחֹדֶשׁ הָרִאשׁוֹן בְּאַרְבָּעָה עָשָׂר לַחֹדֶשׁ בֵּין הָעַרְבַּיִם פֶּסַח לַיהֹוָה:

במדבר ט:א-יד

וַיְדַבֵּר יְהֹוָה אֶל מֹשֶׁה בְמִדְבַּר סִינַי בַּשָּׁנָה הַשֵּׁנִית לְצֵאתָם מֵאֶרֶץ מִצְרַיִם בַּחֹדֶשׁ הָרִאשׁוֹן לֵאמֹר: וְיַעֲשׂוּ בְנֵי יִשְׂרָאֵל אֶת הַפָּסַח בְּמוֹעֲדוֹ: בְּאַרְבָּעָה עָשָׂר יוֹם בַּחֹדֶשׁ הַזֶּה בֵּין הָעַרְבַּיִם תַּעֲשׂוּ אֹתוֹ בְּמוֹעֲדוֹ כְּכָל חֻקֹּתָיו וּכְכָל מִשְׁפָּטָיו תַּעֲשׂוּ אֹתוֹ: וַיְדַבֵּר מֹשֶׁה אֶל בְּנֵי יִשְׂרָאֵל לַעֲשֹׂת הַפָּסַח: וַיַּעֲשׂוּ אֶת הַפֶּסַח בָּרִאשׁוֹן בְּאַרְבָּעָה עָשָׂר יוֹם לַחֹדֶשׁ בֵּין הָעַרְבַּיִם בְּמִדְבַּר סִינָי כְּכֹל אֲשֶׁר צִוָּה יְהֹוָה אֶת מֹשֶׁה כֵּן עָשׂוּ בְּנֵי יִשְׂרָאֵל: וַיְהִי אֲנָשִׁים אֲשֶׁר הָיוּ טְמֵאִים לְנֶפֶשׁ אָדָם וְלֹא יָכְלוּ לַעֲשֹׂת הַפֶּסַח בַּיּוֹם הַהוּא וַיִּקְרְבוּ לִפְנֵי מֹשֶׁה וְלִפְנֵי אַהֲרֹן בַּיּוֹם הַהוּא: וַיֹּאמְרוּ הָאֲנָשִׁים הָהֵמָּה אֵלָיו אֲנַחְנוּ טְמֵאִים לְנֶפֶשׁ אָדָם לָמָּה נִגָּרַע לְבִלְתִּי הַקְרִיב אֶת קָרְבַּן יְהֹוָה בְּמֹעֲדוֹ בְּתוֹךְ בְּנֵי יִשְׂרָאֵל: וַיֹּאמֶר אֲלֵהֶם מֹשֶׁה עִמְדוּ וְאֶשְׁמְעָה מַה יְצַוֶּה יְהֹוָה לָכֶם:

וַיְדַבֵּר יְהֹוָה אֶל מֹשֶׁה לֵּאמֹר: דַּבֵּר אֶל בְּנֵי יִשְׂרָאֵל

לֵאמֹר אִישׁ אִישׁ כִּי יִהְיֶה טָמֵא לָנֶפֶשׁ אוֹ בְדֶרֶךְ רְחֹקָה לָכֶם אוֹ לְדֹרֹתֵיכֶם וְעָשָׂה פֶסַח לַיהֹוָה: בַּחֹדֶשׁ הַשֵּׁנִי בְּאַרְבָּעָה עָשָׂר יוֹם בֵּין הָעַרְבַּיִם יַעֲשׂוּ אֹתוֹ עַל מַצּוֹת וּמְרֹרִים יֹאכְלֻהוּ: לֹא יַשְׁאִירוּ מִמֶּנּוּ עַד בֹּקֶר וְעֶצֶם לֹא יִשְׁבְּרוּ בוֹ כְּכָל חֻקַּת הַפֶּסַח יַעֲשׂוּ אֹתוֹ: וְהָאִישׁ אֲשֶׁר הוּא טָהוֹר וּבְדֶרֶךְ לֹא הָיָה וְחָדַל לַעֲשׂוֹת הַפֶּסַח וְנִכְרְתָה הַנֶּפֶשׁ הַהִוא מֵעַמֶּיהָ כִּי קָרְבַּן יְהֹוָה לֹא הִקְרִיב בְּמֹעֲדוֹ חֶטְאוֹ יִשָּׂא הָאִישׁ הַהוּא: וְכִי יָגוּר אִתְּכֶם גֵּר וְעָשָׂה פֶסַח לַיהֹוָה כְּחֻקַּת הַפֶּסַח וּכְמִשְׁפָּטוֹ כֵּן יַעֲשֶׂה חֻקָּה אַחַת יִהְיֶה לָכֶם וְלַגֵּר וּלְאֶזְרַח הָאָרֶץ:

במדבר כח:טז

וּבַחֹדֶשׁ הָרִאשׁוֹן בְּאַרְבָּעָה עָשָׂר יוֹם לַחֹדֶשׁ פֶּסַח לַיהֹוָה:

דברים טז:א-ח

שָׁמוֹר אֶת חֹדֶשׁ הָאָבִיב וְעָשִׂיתָ פֶּסַח לַיהֹוָה אֱלֹהֶיךָ כִּי בְּחֹדֶשׁ הָאָבִיב הוֹצִיאֲךָ יְהֹוָה אֱלֹהֶיךָ מִמִּצְרַיִם לָיְלָה: וְזָבַחְתָּ פֶּסַח לַיהֹוָה אֱלֹהֶיךָ צֹאן

וּבָקָר בַּמָּקוֹם אֲשֶׁר יִבְחַר יְהוָה לְשַׁכֵּן שְׁמוֹ שָׁם:
לֹא תֹאכַל עָלָיו חָמֵץ שִׁבְעַת יָמִים תֹּאכַל עָלָיו
מַצּוֹת לֶחֶם עֹנִי כִּי בְחִפָּזוֹן יָצָאתָ מֵאֶרֶץ מִצְרַיִם
לְמַעַן תִּזְכֹּר אֶת יוֹם צֵאתְךָ מֵאֶרֶץ מִצְרַיִם כֹּל
יְמֵי חַיֶּיךָ: וְלֹא יֵרָאֶה לְךָ שְׂאֹר בְּכָל גְּבֻלְךָ שִׁבְעַת
יָמִים וְלֹא יָלִין מִן הַבָּשָׂר אֲשֶׁר תִּזְבַּח בָּעֶרֶב בַּיּוֹם
הָרִאשׁוֹן לַבֹּקֶר: לֹא תוּכַל לִזְבֹּחַ אֶת הַפָּסַח
בְּאַחַד שְׁעָרֶיךָ אֲשֶׁר יְהוָה אֱלֹהֶיךָ נֹתֵן לָךְ: כִּי
אִם אֶל הַמָּקוֹם אֲשֶׁר יִבְחַר יְהוָה אֱלֹהֶיךָ לְשַׁכֵּן
שְׁמוֹ שָׁם תִּזְבַּח אֶת הַפֶּסַח בָּעָרֶב כְּבוֹא הַשֶּׁמֶשׁ
מוֹעֵד צֵאתְךָ מִמִּצְרָיִם: וּבִשַּׁלְתָּ וְאָכַלְתָּ בַּמָּקוֹם
אֲשֶׁר יִבְחַר יְהוָה אֱלֹהֶיךָ בּוֹ וּפָנִיתָ בַבֹּקֶר וְהָלַכְתָּ
לְאֹהָלֶיךָ: שֵׁשֶׁת יָמִים תֹּאכַל מַצּוֹת וּבַיּוֹם הַשְּׁבִיעִי
עֲצֶרֶת לַיהוָה אֱלֹהֶיךָ לֹא תַעֲשֶׂה מְלָאכָה:

יהושע ה: י-יא

וַיַּחֲנוּ בְנֵי יִשְׂרָאֵל בַּגִּלְגָּל וַיַּעֲשׂוּ אֶת הַפֶּסַח
בְּאַרְבָּעָה עָשָׂר יוֹם לַחֹדֶשׁ בָּעֶרֶב בְּעַרְבוֹת יְרִיחוֹ:
וַיֹּאכְלוּ מֵעֲבוּר הָאָרֶץ מִמָּחֳרַת הַפֶּסַח מַצּוֹת
וְקָלוּי בְּעֶצֶם הַיּוֹם הַזֶּה:

מלכים ב כג:כא-כג

וַיְצַו הַמֶּלֶךְ אֶת כָּל הָעָם לֵאמֹר עֲשׂוּ פֶסַח לַיהוָה
אֱלֹהֵיכֶם כַּכָּתוּב עַל סֵפֶר הַבְּרִית הַזֶּה: כִּי לֹא
נַעֲשָׂה כַּפֶּסַח הַזֶּה מִימֵי הַשֹּׁפְטִים אֲשֶׁר שָׁפְטוּ
אֶת יִשְׂרָאֵל וְכֹל יְמֵי מַלְכֵי יִשְׂרָאֵל וּמַלְכֵי יְהוּדָה:
כִּי אִם בִּשְׁמֹנֶה עֶשְׂרֵה שָׁנָה לַמֶּלֶךְ יֹאשִׁיָּהוּ נַעֲשָׂה
הַפֶּסַח הַזֶּה לַיהוָה בִּירוּשָׁלָ‍ִם:

דברי הימים ב ל:א-כ

וַיִּשְׁלַח יְחִזְקִיָּהוּ עַל כָּל יִשְׂרָאֵל וִיהוּדָה וְגַם
אִגְּרוֹת כָּתַב עַל אֶפְרַיִם וּמְנַשֶּׁה לָבוֹא לְבֵית יְהוָה
בִּירוּשָׁלַ‍ִם לַעֲשׂוֹת פֶּסַח לַיהוָה אֱלֹהֵי יִשְׂרָאֵל:
וַיִּוָּעַץ הַמֶּלֶךְ וְשָׂרָיו וְכָל הַקָּהָל בִּירוּשָׁלַ‍ִם לַעֲשׂוֹת
הַפֶּסַח בַּחֹדֶשׁ הַשֵּׁנִי: כִּי לֹא יָכְלוּ לַעֲשֹׂתוֹ בָּעֵת
הַהִיא כִּי הַכֹּהֲנִים לֹא הִתְקַדְּשׁוּ לְמַדַּי וְהָעָם
לֹא נֶאֶסְפוּ לִירוּשָׁלָ‍ִם: וַיִּישַׁר הַדָּבָר בְּעֵינֵי הַמֶּלֶךְ
וּבְעֵינֵי כָּל הַקָּהָל: וַיַּעֲמִידוּ דָבָר לְהַעֲבִיר קוֹל
בְּכָל יִשְׂרָאֵל מִבְּאֵר שֶׁבַע וְעַד דָּן לָבוֹא לַעֲשׂוֹת
פֶּסַח לַיהוָה אֱלֹהֵי יִשְׂרָאֵל בִּירוּשָׁלָ‍ִם כִּי לֹא לָרֹב
עָשׂוּ כַּכָּתוּב: וַיֵּלְכוּ הָרָצִים בָּאִגְּרוֹת מִיַּד הַמֶּלֶךְ

וְשָׂרָיו בְּכָל יִשְׂרָאֵל וִיהוּדָה וּכְמִצְוַת הַמֶּלֶךְ לֵאמֹר בְּנֵי יִשְׂרָאֵל שׁוּבוּ אֶל יְהֹוָה אֱלֹהֵי אַבְרָהָם יִצְחָק וְיִשְׂרָאֵל וְיָשֹׁב אֶל הַפְּלֵיטָה הַנִּשְׁאֶרֶת לָכֶם מִכַּף מַלְכֵי אַשּׁוּר: וְאַל תִּהְיוּ כַּאֲבוֹתֵיכֶם וְכַאֲחֵיכֶם אֲשֶׁר מָעֲלוּ בַּיהֹוָה אֱלֹהֵי אֲבוֹתֵיהֶם וַיִּתְּנֵם לְשַׁמָּה כַּאֲשֶׁר אַתֶּם רֹאִים: עַתָּה אַל תַּקְשׁוּ עָרְפְּכֶם כַּאֲבוֹתֵיכֶם תְּנוּ יָד לַיהֹוָה וּבֹאוּ לְמִקְדָּשׁוֹ אֲשֶׁר הִקְדִּישׁ לְעוֹלָם וְעִבְדוּ אֶת יְהֹוָה אֱלֹהֵיכֶם וְיָשֹׁב מִכֶּם חֲרוֹן אַפּוֹ: כִּי בְשׁוּבְכֶם עַל יְהֹוָה אֲחֵיכֶם וּבְנֵיכֶם לְרַחֲמִים לִפְנֵי שׁוֹבֵיהֶם וְלָשׁוּב לָאָרֶץ הַזֹּאת כִּי חַנּוּן וְרַחוּם יְהֹוָה אֱלֹהֵיכֶם וְלֹא יָסִיר פָּנִים מִכֶּם אִם תָּשׁוּבוּ אֵלָיו: וַיִּהְיוּ הָרָצִים עֹבְרִים מֵעִיר לָעִיר בְּאֶרֶץ אֶפְרַיִם וּמְנַשֶּׁה וְעַד זְבֻלוּן וַיִּהְיוּ מַשְׂחִיקִים עֲלֵיהֶם וּמַלְעִגִים בָּם: אַךְ אֲנָשִׁים מֵאָשֵׁר וּמְנַשֶּׁה וּמִזְּבֻלוּן נִכְנְעוּ וַיָּבֹאוּ לִירוּשָׁלָם: גַּם בִּיהוּדָה הָיְתָה יַד הָאֱלֹהִים לָתֵת לָהֶם לֵב אֶחָד לַעֲשׂוֹת מִצְוַת הַמֶּלֶךְ וְהַשָּׂרִים בִּדְבַר יְהֹוָה: וַיֵּאָסְפוּ יְרוּשָׁלַם עַם רָב לַעֲשׂוֹת אֶת חַג הַמַּצּוֹת בַּחֹדֶשׁ הַשֵּׁנִי קָהָל לָרֹב מְאֹד: וַיָּקֻמוּ וַיָּסִירוּ אֶת הַמִּזְבְּחוֹת אֲשֶׁר בִּירוּשָׁלָם וְאֵת כָּל הַמְקַטְּרוֹת

הֵסִירוּ וַיַּשְׁלִיכוּ לְנַחַל קִדְרוֹן: וַיִּשְׁחֲטוּ הַפֶּסַח בְּאַרְבָּעָה עָשָׂר לַחֹדֶשׁ הַשֵּׁנִי וְהַכֹּהֲנִים וְהַלְוִיִּם נִכְלְמוּ וַיִּתְקַדְּשׁוּ וַיָּבִיאוּ עֹלוֹת בֵּית יְהֹוָה: וַיַּעַמְדוּ עַל עָמְדָם כְּמִשְׁפָּטָם כְּתוֹרַת מֹשֶׁה אִישׁ הָאֱלֹהִים הַכֹּהֲנִים זֹרְקִים אֶת הַדָּם מִיַּד הַלְוִיִּם: כִּי רַבַּת בַּקָּהָל אֲשֶׁר לֹא הִתְקַדָּשׁוּ וְהַלְוִיִּם עַל שְׁחִיטַת הַפְּסָחִים לְכֹל לֹא טָהוֹר לְהַקְדִּישׁ לַיהֹוָה: כִּי מַרְבִּית הָעָם רַבַּת מֵאֶפְרַיִם וּמְנַשֶּׁה יִשָּׂשכָר וּזְבֻלוּן לֹא הִטֶּהָרוּ כִּי אָכְלוּ אֶת הַפֶּסַח בְּלֹא כַכָּתוּב כִּי הִתְפַּלֵּל יְחִזְקִיָּהוּ עֲלֵיהֶם לֵאמֹר יְהֹוָה הַטּוֹב יְכַפֵּר בְּעַד: כָּל לְבָבוֹ הֵכִין לִדְרוֹשׁ הָאֱלֹהִים יְהֹוָה אֱלֹהֵי אֲבוֹתָיו וְלֹא כְּטָהֳרַת הַקֹּדֶשׁ: וַיִּשְׁמַע יְהֹוָה אֶל יְחִזְקִיָּהוּ וַיִּרְפָּא אֶת הָעָם:

דברי הימים ב לה:א-יט

וַיַּעַשׂ יֹאשִׁיָּהוּ בִירוּשָׁלַם פֶּסַח לַיהֹוָה וַיִּשְׁחֲטוּ הַפֶּסַח בְּאַרְבָּעָה עָשָׂר לַחֹדֶשׁ הָרִאשׁוֹן: וַיַּעֲמֵד הַכֹּהֲנִים עַל מִשְׁמְרוֹתָם וַיְחַזְּקֵם לַעֲבוֹדַת בֵּית יְהֹוָה: וַיֹּאמֶר לַלְוִיִּם הַמְּבִינִים לְכָל יִשְׂרָאֵל הַקְּדוֹשִׁים לַיהֹוָה תְּנוּ אֶת אֲרוֹן הַקֹּדֶשׁ בַּבַּיִת אֲשֶׁר

בָּנָה שְׁלֹמֹה בֶן דָּוִיד מֶלֶךְ יִשְׂרָאֵל אֵין לָכֶם מַשָּׂא
בַּכָּתֵף עַתָּה עִבְדוּ אֶת יְהוָה אֱלֹהֵיכֶם וְאֵת עַמּוֹ
יִשְׂרָאֵל: וְהָכִינוּ לְבֵית אֲבוֹתֵיכֶם כְּמַחְלְקוֹתֵיכֶם
בִּכְתָב דָּוִיד מֶלֶךְ יִשְׂרָאֵל וּבְמִכְתַּב שְׁלֹמֹה בְנוֹ:
וְעִמְדוּ בַקֹּדֶשׁ לִפְלֻגּוֹת בֵּית הָאָבוֹת לַאֲחֵיכֶם בְּנֵי
הָעָם וַחֲלֻקַּת בֵּית אָב לַלְוִיִּם: וְשַׁחֲטוּ הַפָּסַח
וְהִתְקַדְּשׁוּ וְהָכִינוּ לַאֲחֵיכֶם לַעֲשׂוֹת כִּדְבַר יְהוָה
בְּיַד מֹשֶׁה: וַיָּרֶם יֹאשִׁיָּהוּ לִבְנֵי הָעָם צֹאן כְּבָשִׂים
וּבְנֵי עִזִּים הַכֹּל לַפְּסָחִים לְכָל הַנִּמְצָא לְמִסְפַּר
שְׁלֹשִׁים אֶלֶף וּבָקָר שְׁלֹשֶׁת אֲלָפִים אֵלֶּה מֵרְכוּשׁ
הַמֶּלֶךְ: וְשָׂרָיו לִנְדָבָה לָעָם לַכֹּהֲנִים וְלַלְוִיִּם הֵרִימוּ
חִלְקִיָּה וּזְכַרְיָהוּ וִיחִיאֵל נְגִידֵי בֵּית הָאֱלֹהִים
לַכֹּהֲנִים נָתְנוּ לַפְּסָחִים אֲלָפִים וְשֵׁשׁ מֵאוֹת וּבָקָר
שְׁלֹשׁ מֵאוֹת: וְכָנַנְיָהוּ וּשְׁמַעְיָהוּ וּנְתַנְאֵל אֶחָיו
וַחֲשַׁבְיָהוּ וִיעִיאֵל וְיוֹזָבָד שָׂרֵי הַלְוִיִּם הֵרִימוּ לַלְוִיִּם
לַפְּסָחִים חֲמֵשֶׁת אֲלָפִים וּבָקָר חֲמֵשׁ מֵאוֹת: וַתִּכּוֹן
הָעֲבוֹדָה וַיַּעַמְדוּ הַכֹּהֲנִים עַל עָמְדָם וְהַלְוִיִּם
עַל מַחְלְקוֹתָם כְּמִצְוַת הַמֶּלֶךְ: וַיִּשְׁחֲטוּ הַפָּסַח
וַיִּזְרְקוּ הַכֹּהֲנִים מִיָּדָם וְהַלְוִיִּם מַפְשִׁיטִים: וַיָּסִירוּ

הָעֹלָה לְתִתָּם לְמִפְלַגּוֹת לְבֵית אָבוֹת לִבְנֵי הָעָם
לְהַקְרִיב לַיהוָה כַּכָּתוּב בְּסֵפֶר מֹשֶׁה וְכֵן לַבָּקָר:
וַיְבַשְּׁלוּ הַפֶּסַח בָּאֵשׁ כַּמִּשְׁפָּט וְהַקֳּדָשִׁים בִּשְּׁלוּ
בַּסִּירוֹת וּבַדְּוָדִים וּבַצֵּלָחוֹת וַיָּרִיצוּ לְכָל בְּנֵי הָעָם:
וְאַחַר הֵכִינוּ לָהֶם וְלַכֹּהֲנִים כִּי הַכֹּהֲנִים בְּנֵי אַהֲרֹן
בְּהַעֲלוֹת הָעוֹלָה וְהַחֲלָבִים עַד לָיְלָה וְהַלְוִיִּם
הֵכִינוּ לָהֶם וְלַכֹּהֲנִים בְּנֵי אַהֲרֹן: וְהַמְשֹׁרְרִים
בְּנֵי אָסָף עַל מַעֲמָדָם כְּמִצְוַת דָּוִיד וְאָסָף וְהֵימָן
וִידֻתוּן חוֹזֵה הַמֶּלֶךְ וְהַשֹּׁעֲרִים לְשַׁעַר וָשָׁעַר אֵין
לָהֶם לָסוּר מֵעַל עֲבֹדָתָם כִּי אֲחֵיהֶם הַלְוִיִּם הֵכִינוּ
לָהֶם: וַתִּכּוֹן כָּל עֲבוֹדַת יְהוָה בַּיּוֹם הַהוּא לַעֲשׂוֹת
הַפֶּסַח וְהַעֲלוֹת עֹלוֹת עַל מִזְבַּח יְהוָה כְּמִצְוַת
הַמֶּלֶךְ יֹאשִׁיָּהוּ: וַיַּעֲשׂוּ בְנֵי יִשְׂרָאֵל הַנִּמְצְאִים
אֶת הַפֶּסַח בָּעֵת הַהִיא וְאֶת חַג הַמַּצּוֹת שִׁבְעַת
יָמִים: וְלֹא נַעֲשָׂה פֶסַח כָּמֹהוּ בְּיִשְׂרָאֵל מִימֵי
שְׁמוּאֵל הַנָּבִיא וְכָל מַלְכֵי יִשְׂרָאֵל לֹא עָשׂוּ כַּפֶּסַח
אֲשֶׁר עָשָׂה יֹאשִׁיָּהוּ וְהַכֹּהֲנִים וְהַלְוִיִּם וְכָל יְהוּדָה
וְיִשְׂרָאֵל הַנִּמְצָא וְיוֹשְׁבֵי יְרוּשָׁלָ͏ִם: בִּשְׁמוֹנֶה עֶשְׂרֵה
שָׁנָה לְמַלְכוּת יֹאשִׁיָּהוּ נַעֲשָׂה הַפֶּסַח הַזֶּה:

Chapter Four
Eiruv Tavshilin

The following is a brief summary of the laws applicable specifically for Pesach.
For a comprehensive discussion of the topic, see Guidelines to Yom Tov.

88. When Yom Tov is on Friday (e.g. 7th day Pesach), or on Thursday and Friday (1st and 2nd days in *Chutz La'aretz*), one is required to prepare food before Yom Tov especially for Shabbos. This food is called *Eiruv Tavshilin*.

89. It is usually forbidden to make any preparations on Yom Tov for the following day. However, if one began to prepare for Shabbos before Yom Tov, he may finish the preparations on Yom Tov that is Friday. The *Eiruv Tavshilin* foods are considered to be the start of the preparations.

90. The *eiruv* permits all activities that are permitted on Yom Tov, e.g. cooking, grinding, sorting. Activities that are forbidden on Yom Tov, such as turning on lights, do not become permitted due to the *eiruv*.

91. It is usually sufficient for the head of the household to make an *Eiruv Tavshillin*. This automatically allows the wife and children to make preparations on Yom Tov for Shabbos.

92. A person who does not intend making any preparations on Friday for Shabbos and does not need to kindle Shabbos lights does not require an *Eiruv Tavshilin*. A person who needs only to kindle Shabbos lights should make an *eiruv* without a *b'racha*. This may be relevant for a person who is staying in a hotel or is invited out for all the Shabbos meals.

93. A visitor is not automatically included in the host's *eiruv*. Therefore, he must make his own *eiruv* if he intends to do some Shabbos preparations on Friday. Alternatively, he can become a partner in the family *eiruv*.

The Guidelines Haggadah

94. The custom is that visiting married children do not make their own *eiruv* but rely on the family one.

95. Visitors in *Chutz La'aretz* from *Eretz Yisroel* do not need to make an *Eiruv Tavshilin* when the first day of Pesach is on Thursday. When the seventh day is on Friday, everyone must make an *Eiruv Tavshilin*.

96. Visitors in *Eretz Yisroel* from *Chutz La'aretz* need to make an *Eiruv Tavshilin* when the first day of Pesach is on Thursday. Although a guest is usually included with the *eiruv* of his host, in this situation he must make his own *eiruv*. When the seventh day is on Friday, everyone must make an *Eiruv Tavshilin*.

97. Ideally, one should make the *eiruv* on *erev Yom Tov*. If necessary, it may be made on the night preceding *erev Yom Tov* and in extenuating circumstances even on an earlier day.

98. It is advisable for notices to be posted in shuls to remind people to perform this mitzvah.

99. The *eiruv* should preferably be made before the Yom Tov lights are kindled. If one forgot, he may make it until nightfall.

100. A cooked food and a baked food should be used for the *eiruv*. The custom is to take meat, poultry, fish, or egg for the cooked food and a whole matza for the baked food. It is also permitted to use a roasted or fried food for the cooked food.

101. In former times, the common practice was to use a hard-boiled egg for the cooked food since this would certainly last for several days without spoiling. Today, when refrigerators are available, one should beautify the mitzvah by using a more superior type of food, e.g. a portion of chicken or fish.

102. If one does not have any fresh food, one may use frozen food that is fully cooked.

103. The cooked food must be a *kezayis* and the baked food should preferably be a *kebeitza*. These quantities are sufficient even if the *eiruv* is being made on behalf of many people.

104. One may not use a cooked food that is not usually served at a main course of a bread meal, e.g. cooked fruit.

105. It is not necessary to cook the food personally, and one may use bought food.

However, it is a greater mitzvah to personally prepare the food specifically for the *eiruv*.

106. One may not eat the *eiruv* foods on Yom Tov. The foods must be kept in a safe place until Shabbos. Since the cooked food is usually kept in the fridge, it should be wrapped and labeled clearly to prevent people from accidentally eating it.

107. The food should be eaten on Shabbos. The custom is to use the matza for *Lechem Mishneh* at each of the Shabbos meals and to eat it at *Seuda Shelishis*. The cooked food should preferably be eaten on Friday night.

108. If a person did not know that he had to make an *eiruv* or if he forgot to make one, he may rely on the *eiruv* of the rav. Similarly, if he knew about the concept of *Eiruv Tavshilin* but thought that he may rely upon the rav's eiruv, he is included in the *eiruv* of the rav.

109. When an *eiruv* is made, one should make every effort to complete the preparations early enough on Friday afternoon that the food will be edible well before Shabbos. Similarly, water should be put on the stove so that it boils well before Shabbos. Nevertheless, if the preparations were left until late on Friday afternoon, they may still be done.

110. The *eiruv* only permits one to prepare on Friday for Shabbos, but not on Thursday which is Yom Tov. Even if a person knows that he will be unable to prepare on Friday and makes the *eiruv* with this in mind, he may not cook on Thursday for Shabbos. Preparations may begin on Thursday night.

> *The eiruv foods should be held while the b'racha and eiruv declaration are recited.*

Blessed are You, Hashem our God, King of the universe, Who has sanctified us with His commandments and commanded us to perform the mitzva of *eiruv*.

By means of these *eiruv* foods, we will be permitted to bake, cook, keep foods warm, light candles, carry, and do all that we need on Yom Tov for Shabbos.

בָּרוּךְ אַתָּה יְיָ אֱלֹהֵינוּ מֶלֶךְ הָעוֹלָם, אֲשֶׁר קִדְּשָׁנוּ בְּמִצְוֹתָיו, וְצִוָּנוּ עַל מִצְוַת עֵרוּב:

בְּהָדֵין עֵירוּבָא יְהֵא שָׁרֵא לָנָא לַאֲפוּיֵי וּלְבַשּׁוּלֵי וּלְאַטְמוּנֵי וּלְאַדְלוּקֵי שְׁרָגָא וּלְאַפּוּקֵי וּלְמֶעְבַּד כָּל צָרְכָנָא מִיּוֹמָא טָבָא לְשַׁבַּתָּא:

> *The declaration must be said in a language that one understands.*
> *If one does not understand the Aramaic words, he should say the translation.*

Chapter Five

Candle Lighting

The following is a brief summary of the laws.
For a comprehensive discussion of the topic, see Guidelines to Yom Tov.

111. Two lights are kindled on *erev Pesach* as for Shabbos. Those who have the custom to kindle additional lights for Shabbos usually do the same for Yom Tov.

112. The wife should kindle the lights as on *erev Shabbos*.

113. In *Chutz La'aretz*, all the lights that will be needed for both days of Yom Tov should preferably be prepared in advance. If this was not done, the lights for the second night may be prepared only after nightfall following the first day.

114. Since there is a mitzvah for the lights to be burning during the meal, care should be taken on the Seder night(s) to use long candles or a sufficient amount of oil.

115. When preparing the lights for the second night, one may scrape out with a knife any wax that remains in the bottom of the candlesticks. The new candles may be pushed into the candlesticks but must not be melted in.

116. It is permitted to insert a wick into a floating disc, but a hole must not be made in the middle of the disc.

117. Some candles have a small circular metal disc that remains in the bottom of the glass. This disc may be removed to allow new candles to be placed inside.

118. Cotton wool may not be torn or twisted to form a wick. Wicks must not be cut to size.

119. When Pesach is on Sunday, one should not reuse wicks that were lit for the first time for

Shabbos. The wicks may be used if they were lit on a prior occasion, or singed on *erev Shabbos* (as many have the custom to do). New wicks may be used.

120. The Yom Tov lights should preferably be kindled before sunset as on *erev Shabbos*, but if one is pressed for time he may light them later in the evening.

121. The lights for the second night of Yom Tov may be kindled only after nightfall. The same applies on the eighth night.

122. When the seventh day of Pesach is on Friday, the Shabbos lights must be kindled on Friday afternoon before sunset. The same applies in *Chutz La'aretz* when the second day is Friday.

123. When the second day is Sunday, one must say *baruch hamavdil bein kodesh le'kodesh* (or recite *Vatodi'einu* during *Ma'ariv*) before lighting on the second night. On other days, nothing need be said.

124. Although for Shabbos the lights are kindled first and then the *b'racha* recited, for Yom Tov the order is reversed and the *brachos* are recited before kindling. Some have the custom to follow the same order as for Shabbos, i.e. to kindle the lights and then recite the *brachos*.

125. When the lights are kindled after nightfall, the *brachos* should be recited first, according to both customs. Nevertheless, some still maintain their custom to kindle the lights first.

126. When Yom Tov is on Shabbos, the lights must be kindled first and then the *brachos* recited as is usual for Shabbos.

127. If one is kindling on the first or seventh night before sunset and wishes to kindle after reciting the *brachos*, one should be aware of the following: Since it is forbidden to kindle a new flame after reciting the *brachos*, a candle, match, or taper should be lit beforehand. After the lights have been kindled, the match etc. may not be blown or shaken out, but it must be put down carefully and left to burn out by itself. One need not place the hands in front of the eyes as is done when kindling before reciting the *b'racha*.

128. If one is lighting on the first or seventh night after sunset, the lights must be kindled from an existing flame. The lights should be kindled with an intermediary candle, match, or taper, rather than the lights themselves taken to the existing flame. The match etc. may not be

blown or shaken out, but it must be put down carefully and left to burn out by itself. These rules also apply when lighting on the second and eighth night and on Friday afternoon when Yom Tov is Friday.

129. A woman should answer amen to the *b'racha Shehecheyanu* that she hears during Kiddush, even if she recited it when lighting candles.

130. A woman who intends to recite Kiddush should preferably recite the *b'racha Shehecheyanu* then and not when lighting candles.

131. The *b'racha Shehecheyanu* is not recited on the seventh and eighth days of Pesach.

132. A woman who forgot to kindle lights on Yom Tov is not penalized.

When Yom Tov is on a weekday, the following brachos are recited. Shehecheyanu is recited in Chutz La'aretz on both Seder nights.

Blessed are You, Hashem our God, King of the universe, Who has sanctified us with His commandments and commanded us to kindle the light of Yom Tov.

בָּרוּךְ אַתָּה יְיָ אֱלֹהֵינוּ מֶלֶךְ הָעוֹלָם, אֲשֶׁר קִדְּשָׁנוּ בְּמִצְוֹתָיו, וְצִוָּנוּ לְהַדְלִיק נֵר שֶׁל יוֹם טוֹב:

Blessed are You, Hashem our God, King of the universe, Who has kept us alive, sustained us, and brought us to this season.

בָּרוּךְ אַתָּה יְיָ אֱלֹהֵינוּ מֶלֶךְ הָעוֹלָם, שֶׁהֶחֱיָנוּ וְקִיְּמָנוּ וְהִגִּיעָנוּ לַזְּמַן הַזֶּה:

The Guidelines Haggadah   36

When Yom Tov is on Shabbos, the following brachos are recited:

Blessed are You, Hashem our God, King of the universe, Who has sanctified us with His commandments and commanded us to kindle the light of Shabbos and Yom Tov.

בָּרוּךְ אַתָּה יְיָ אֱלֹהֵינוּ מֶלֶךְ הָעוֹלָם, אֲשֶׁר קִדְּשָׁנוּ בְּמִצְוֹתָיו, וְצִוָּנוּ לְהַדְלִיק נֵר שֶׁל שַׁבָּת וְשֶׁל יוֹם טוֹב:

Blessed are You, Hashem our God, King of the universe, Who has kept us alive, sustained us, and brought us to this season.

בָּרוּךְ אַתָּה יְיָ אֱלֹהֵינוּ מֶלֶךְ הָעוֹלָם, שֶׁהֶחֱיָנוּ וְקִיְּמָנוּ וְהִגִּיעָנוּ לַזְּמַן הַזֶּה:

Chapter Six

Preparations for the Seder

The Wine and the Cup

133.   Drinking four cups of wine is a Rabbinic mitzvah that demonstrates our freedom since wine is the drink of free men and nobility. The four cups correspond to the four terms of redemption used by Hashem when He promised to redeem the Jewish people from the bondage in *Mitzrayim* (*Shemos* 6:6-7).

134.   Red wine is preferred for two reasons. The red color indicates the wine's superiority and it is a reminder of the Jewish blood that was shed.

135.   One may use white wine if it is of better quality, but it is preferable to mix it with a little red wine to give it a red color. One should

preferably pour the white wine into the red wine when mixing on Yom Tov.

136.   Carbonated (sparkling) wine may be used if it tastes like wine.

137.   A person who has difficulty drinking wine may use a type that has a low alcohol content. Alternatively, he may mix wine and grape juice, taking care that there is still a taste of wine. One should be wary about diluting wine with water since such a mixture may be invalid. Whoever exerts himself to drink the four cups of wine and eat the correct quantities of matza even if he finds it difficult will be spared from having to eat and drink bitter medicines. However, a

person is not required to drink wine if it will make him ill.

138. A person who cannot tolerate even weak wine may use grape juice. Nevertheless, it is better to use a small cup of weak wine than a large cup of grape juice (see no. 141).

139. One should avoid switching wines during the Seder since a change from an inferior wine to a superior one may require a special *b'racha* (*Hatov Vehameitiv*). Therefore, a person should select the type of wine that he will enjoy drinking and use it for all four cups. Alternatively, all the different wines should be placed on the table at the start of the Seder. This mitigates the need for the special *b'racha*.

140. A person who cannot tolerate either wine or grape juice should use a drink that is considered to be a national beverage. A rav should be consulted to ascertain which drinks qualify for this purpose. In this situation, the *b'racha Shehakol* should be recited instead of *Borei Pri Hagafen* and only for the first and third cups.

141. According to the two main opinions, the cup must hold at least 86cc (approx. 3 fl. oz) or 150cc (approx. 5 fl. oz). Since the mitzva of drinking four cups of wine is Rabbinic, one may be lenient to use the smaller quantity. When the Seder is on Friday night, the first cup (Kiddush) is a Torah mitzvah and one is recommended to use the larger quantity. In any event, one should use a cup that holds slightly more than the minimum quantity since wine often spills when holding the cup and when reclining.

142. Ideally, one should drink the entire cup even if it contains more than the required amount. If this is not possible, it is sufficient to drink the majority of the cup. Therefore, it is better to use a small cup containing the minimum quantity that can be finished rather than a large cup that cannot be finished.

143. One must not use *shemittah* wine or grape juice at the Seder. This is because it is forbidden to waste *shemittah* wine and the custom is not to drink the wine that is spilled at the ten plagues. In addition, wine often spills during the Seder and this would also be wasted.

144. The leader of the Seder should not pour his own cup, but another person should pour for him since being served is a sign of freedom and nobility. Some have the custom that no one pours his own cup.

The Matza

145. The Torah commands that matza must be prepared under constant supervision to prevent it from becoming chametz. Matza is called *Shemura* if it is also made with the intention that it will be used to fulfill the mitzvah of eating matza on the Seder night (לשם מצת מצוה). Regular matza is not made with this additional intention.

146. Only *shemura* matza is acceptable for the Seder.

147. There is much controversy whether *shemura* machine matza is acceptable for the Seder. According to some opinions, it is sufficient for the person who switches on the machine to have the correct intention. According to other opinions, this is not sufficient and machine matzos are invalid. One should follow the traditional custom to use handmade matzos unless one has great difficulty in obtaining or eating such matzos.

148. *Shemura* hand matzos are available in two types - those made from flour that is ground by hand and those made from flour ground by machine. Although some opinions disqualify the use of machinery for baking (see above),

most opinions allow machinery to be used to grind the flour. The custom is to consider the machine-ground type just as acceptable, but it is praiseworthy to use matzos made from hand-ground flour.

149. It is praiseworthy to eat only *shemura* matzos for the entire Pesach for two reasons. First, some opinions require that the matzos for the entire Pesach be prepared with the same intention as those made for the Seder (לשם מצת מצוה). Second, *shemura* matza is usually supervised from the time that the grain is harvested. This is a higher degree of supervision than for regular matza, which is supervised only from the time of grinding.

150. The quantity required for the mitzvah of eating matza is a volume measure called a *kezayis*. The two widely accepted opinions regarding this measure are 30cc. and 50cc. When these figures are converted into weights, the measurements for a *kezayis* of matza are approximately 15 grams and 25 grams. There is little difference between hand matza and machine matza.

151. When performing a Torah obligation, one

should preferably follow the stricter opinion (25 grams) and for a Rabbinic mitzvah one may follow the lenient opinion (15 grams). In extenuating circumstances, one may be lenient to use smaller figures: 17 grams for a Torah obligation and 10 grams for a Rabbinic obligation, e.g. for a sick or elderly person who finds it difficult to eat matza.

152. There is a mitzvah to eat matza three times during the Seder.
   (i) The first *kezayis* of *Hamotzi*. This is a Torah obligation.
   (ii) *Korech*. This is a Rabbinic obligation.
   (iii) *Afikoman*. This is a Rabbinic obligation. The requirement is to eat one *kezayis*, but it is praiseworthy to eat two *kezaysim*.

153. At the second seder in *Chutz La'aretz*, the first *kezayis* is also Rabbinic.

154. The following chart summarizes the required quantities:

155. It is advisable to eat slightly more than these quantities for two reasons. First, the figures are approximate and matzos vary in thickness. Second, some matza is not eaten but falls to the floor or remains between the teeth, and this cannot be included in the quantity.

156. The weight of an average hand matza is usually between 50 and 80 grams. To calculate the approximate weight of a matza one could divide the weight of the matzos in the box by the number of matzos.

157. Machine matzos weigh approx. 30 grams.

158. Although weighing is usually forbidden on Shabbos and Yom Tov, it is permitted for a mitzvah. A regular (spring) scale may be used but not a digital (battery or electric) scale. However, it is recommended that one weigh the matzos before Yom Tov in order to save time and frustration during the Seder. It is also advisable to prepare in advance pieces of matza

	First seder	Second seder	In case of difficulty or extenuating circumstances
Hamotzi	25g	15g	17g (10g at the second seder)
Korech	15g	15g	10g
Afikoman	30g or 15g	30g or 15g	10g
Total	70g	60g	37g (30g at the second seder)

of matza weighing 10, 15 and 25 grams in separate bags so that they can be distributed during the Seder without delay.

159. According to most opinions, it is not necessary for each person to make an acquisition on the matzos that he intends to eat at the Seder.

The *Maror*

160. Although *Chazal* list five types of *Maror*, the tradition has become unclear as to which species are intended. Only two are definitely known – lettuce and horseradish – and according to some opinions, a third is known to be endives. The widespread custom is to use lettuce or horseradish. According to most opinions, one may use lettuce even if it has no bitterness.

161. Lettuce is the most preferred species. However, there is a major problem that small insects are often found in lettuce and an experienced person must check the leaves. Today, insect-free lettuce is grown in greenhouses under special conditions, and this is obviously the best choice. (It should be rinsed well and checked minimally.) If a person can obtain only regular lettuce and he is afraid that it will not be checked meticulously, he should use the stems and/or hearts. Alternatively, he should use horseradish, which is the second best species.

162. If lettuce is used for *Maror*, one should take a leaf that measures 12" long and 5½" at the widest point. If grated horseradish is used, one should eat 27cc if possible. If this is difficult, it is sufficient to eat 17cc (approx. one heaped tablespoon).

163. In order to keep the lettuce fresh, it may be left in water, but not for a continuous period of twenty-four hours. Lettuce will remain fresh for several days if kept in the fridge.

164. Horseradish must not be eaten whole since this is dangerous. It should be grated on *erev Pesach* in order to release some of its sharpness and kept in a closed container until the Seder. Grated horseradish that is mixed with beetroot juice (commonly called chrain) may not be used for *Maror*.

The Seder Plate

165.   Seven items should be placed on the Seder plate:

1.   Three whole matzos.

2.   A piece of roast meat or poultry.

3.   A hard-boiled or roasted egg.

4.-5. Two portions of *Maror*.

6.   *Charoses*.

7.   *Karpas*.

166.   It is advisable to select a large matza for the middle matza since it is to be divided and the smaller piece should preferably be a *kezayis*.

167.   In addition, salt water should be prepared, but the custom is not to place it on the Seder plate.

168.   If a person has only two whole matzos (besides broken ones), he should use a broken one for the middle matza since this is anyway broken at *Yachatz*.

169.   Although there are several customs regarding the arrangement for the Seder plate,

the most widespread is according to the Arizal. The arrangement is as follows:

170.   If one owns a purpose-built Seder plate, the three matzos should be placed beneath these items. If not, the matzos should be placed on one plate and the remaining items on another plate nearby.

171.   Only the head of the household requires a Seder plate.

172. The far portion of *Maror* is used when the *Maror* is eaten the first time. The near portion is used when eating it the second time together with matza (*Korech*), and is usually referred to as *Chazeres*. The same species of *Maror* may be used for both portions.

173. The meat should preferably be the shankbone, which is from the foreleg of the animal. If poultry is used, the custom is to use the wing or neck. If these are not available, any portion of roast meat or poultry may be used.

174. If one forgot to roast it before Yom Tov, it may be roasted on Yom Tov in the evening, but extra care must be taken to ensure that it is eaten during the day of Yom Tov. If Yom Tov is on Shabbos, it may not be roasted in the evening.

175. The main custom is to roast the egg, although a hard-boiled one is also suitable. Some boil it and then roast it partially.

176. The custom is to leave the egg on the Seder plate in its shell.

177. The custom is to eat the egg during the Seder. Although it is forbidden to eat roast meat or poultry during the Seder, it is permitted to eat roasted eggs.

178. *Charoses* is a mixture of finely chopped fruits, spices, and red wine. Traditionally, the fruits used are sour apples and nuts (particularly almonds) and the spices are cinnamon and ginger. Ideally, the spices should be fine strands to resemble the straw used in *Mitzrayim* to make the mortar.

179. *Karpas* is a vegetable. Ideally, it should be one that is usually eaten raw. The most commonly used are celery, radish, and cabbage. Some use potato, although it is eaten only cooked. (Celery and cabbage should be checked for insects.) Lettuce should not be used since one may not use a vegetable that qualifies as *Maror*.

Reclining

180. One of the four questions asked by the child (*Ma Nishtana*) is why we recline at certain parts of the Seder. The answer is that every person is required to feel on the night of Pesach as though he personally was a slave in *Mitzrayim* and has just been granted his freedom. This mitzvah is one of the greatest challenges of the evening. While reciting the Haggadah and describing the exceedingly torturous oppression and the excruciating persecutions of the Jewish people, a person must use his imagination to visualize himself in *Mitzrayim* enduring the tyrannical slavery. When the discussion turns to the miraculous events of *Yetziyas Mitzrayim*, he must picture himself actually leaving *Mitzrayim* to become a free man. Therefore, when he eats and drinks on this night, he is required to recline in order to demonstrate his newly gained freedom.

181. The custom is that women do not recline. However, in order to demonstrate their feelings of freedom, they should sit in an armchair or a very comfortable chair.

182. Boys aged nine or ten should be trained to recline. According to some opinions, they should be trained from the age of six.

183. A mourner is obligated to recline but he should not sit on an elegant chair.

184. Ideally, one should sit in an armchair or on a chair with armrests and lean to the left side. Preferably, a pillow or cushion should also be placed on the left side of the chair to support the body while reclining. This adds to the feeling of comfort and freedom.

185. If he has only a regular chair, he should recline on the table or on a second chair placed to his left. Alternatively, he may sit sideways and recline on the back of the chair. If possible, he should use a pillow or cushion to create a comfortable position. A person does not fulfill the mitzvah by leaning to the left in mid-air without supporting his body on anything, since this is not the way of free men.

186. He may not lean on his left leg since he would appear to be worried rather than being in a state of happiness. In extenuating circumstances, he may lean on another person's leg.

187. He should not recline on his back or to the right side.

188. A left-handed person should also recline on his left side.

189. The minimum requirement to lean is as follows: when drinking the four cups of wine and when eating the first *kezayis* of matza, the *Korech*, and the *Afikoman*.

190. It is praiseworthy to recline during the entire meal (see no. 337).

191. While reciting the Haggadah, one should sit upright with awe and respect.

General Points

192. At the meal, one must not eat poultry or meat that is prepared without any liquid. This includes roasted, barbecued, and broiled.

193. One may not eat poultry or meat that is roasted in a pot without any liquid. This applies even if it is first cooked with liquid.

194. One may eat poultry or meat that is roasted in a pot with some liquid. This is permitted even if it is first roasted.

195. The main custom is that only the person who leads the Seder wears a *kittel*. In some communities all married men do so.

196. According to the main opinion, a mourner does not wear a *kittel*.

197. The main custom is that a newly wed (in his first year) does wear a *kittel*. (In any case, a newly wed usually celebrates the Seder with his parents or parents-in-law and rarely leads the Seder.)

198. The table should be covered with a white tablecloth. One should place on the table the most exquisite items of silver etc. that he possesses in order to arouse feelings of freedom and royalty. Seating arrangements and preparations for reclining should be organized before Yom Tov so that the Seder can begin as soon as the men arrive home from shul after *Ma'ariv*. Some have the custom to adorn the table with fragrant flowers. The word ריח (fragrance) has the same numerical value (218) as ליל פסח (the evening of Pesach).

199. Before Yom Tov, open all bottles of wine and grape juice and boxes of matza.

200. Rinse all wine cups.

The Guidelines Haggadah

201. Prepare a large and elegant cup for *Eliyahu Hanavi*.

202. Prepare nuts and treats to give to the children before Kiddush and during the Seder.

203. People who bake their own matzos should verify that *challah* has been separated.

204. In *Chutz La'aretz*, *Eiruv Tavshilin* must be made when the first day of Pesach is Thursday.

Chapter Seven

When Pesach falls on Sunday

When the first day of Pesach falls on Motzai Shabbos, there are many changes to the usual sequence of events leading up to Pesach. In order to understand thoroughly the many complex details, one is strongly recommended to attend shiurim or seek expert advice. The following are the most basic rules.

205. The fast of the first-born is on Thursday the twelfth of Nissan. A *Siyum* is held as usual.

206. The search for chametz is performed on Thursday night. The usual *b'racha* is recited and the nullification of chametz is said after the search.

207. The sale of chametz is arranged by the rav during the fifth hour of Friday the thirteenth of Nissan.

208. All unwanted chametz should be burned before the end of the fifth hour on Friday morning. The second nullification is not said until Shabbos morning.

209. Chametz may be eaten all day on Friday. It is an unusual feature of the schedule that one may continue to eat chametz after the unwanted chametz has been burned. However, since the house is already clean for Pesach, it is

recommended that one does not continue to eat chametz all day. No more chametz should be left for eating than is absolutely necessary for the meals on Friday night and Shabbos morning.

210. There are no work restrictions on this Friday. All forms of work including haircuts, laundering, and sewing are permitted.

211. All the preparations for the Seder that are usually made on *erev Pesach* should be made on Friday. Those who use lettuce for *Maror* must not leave it in water for a continuous period of twenty-four hours. Those who use horseradish may either grate it on Friday and keep it in a closed container, or grate it on *motzai Shabbos* in an unusual way.

212. The major challenge is how to eat bread in a house that is clean for Pesach. The simplest and most *halachically* acceptable solution is to eat kosher for Pesach food served on disposable plates. Small challos or pitta bread should be used for *Lechem Mishneh* in order to minimize the quantity of chametz used. Pitta bread has an additional advantage that it does not make many crumbs. After the meal, all unwanted

chametz including crumbs must be destroyed by flushing it down the toilet. Disposable plates to which chametz may be stuck should be taken out of the house and left in a *hefker* place, e.g. public garbage containers (if there is an *eiruv*). In cases of need, any remaining chametz may be removed by a gentile.

213. Opinions differ whether one may eat egg matza instead of bread, and a rav should be consulted.

214. It is forbidden to eat matza on this Shabbos since it is *erev Pesach*. According to the main custom, this includes Friday night. One may be lenient to give matza to children who are below bar or bas mitzvah on Friday night and to very young children on Shabbos morning.

215. On Shabbos morning, one should eat a meal with bread before the deadline time for eating chametz. It is praiseworthy to eat two meals with bread before the deadline with a break in between. Preferably, the break should be half-an-hour, but if one is pressed for time even a shorter interval is sufficient. After the meal(s), the same procedure should

be followed as after the Friday night meal. Teeth should be cleaned with a dry toothbrush without toothpaste or by eating a hard food such as a raw carrot.

216.   The final nullification is said on Shabbos morning after all the remaining chametz has been removed. Special care must be taken to remember to say it before the end of the fifth hour. Since the chametz is not burned, there is a greater likelihood that one may forget to say the nullification.

217.   It is permitted to sleep during the day to have strength for the Seder, but one should not say explicitly that this is why he is sleeping.

When sending the children to bed one must be especially careful not to say that this is in order for them to stay up for the Seder.

218.   One should *daven Mincha* early and then eat a substantial meal (*Seuda Shelishis*) without bread or matza. After the start of the tenth *halachic* hour, foods containing matza meal (e.g. kneidlach) may not be eaten, and other foods may be eaten in moderate amounts.

219.   No preparations may be made for the Seder until *motzai Shabbos*. Women should say *baruch hamavdil bein kodesh lekodesh* before doing any work.

The Guidelines Haggadah

Chapter Eight
The Seder

220. The night of Pesach is indeed very different from all other nights of the year. It is steeped in holiness and abounds with mitzvos, both Torah and Rabbinic, and is rich in customs and traditions. Every detail is of great significance and one should perform each step meticulously knowing that no part of the procedure is trivial. The word 'Seder' means order, indicating that the entire evening follows a set order, arranged by *Chazal* with holy inspiration and invested with hidden meanings and deep interpretations.

221. There are fifteen main steps of the Seder and each one has a special name. These names form a simple rhyme that becomes a memory aid to fulfilling the mitzvos of the evening in the correct order.

*K*adesh, Urchatz, Karpas, Yachatz, Maggid, Rochtza, Motzi, Matza, Maror, Korech, Shulchan Orech, Tzafun, Barech, Hallel, Nirtzah.

קַדֵּשׁ, וּרְחַץ, כַּרְפַּס, יַחַץ,
מַגִּיד, רָחְצָה, מוֹצִיא, מַצָּה,
מָרוֹר, כּוֹרֵךְ, שֻׁלְחָן עוֹרֵךְ,
צָפוּן, בָּרֵךְ, הַלֵּל, נִרְצָה.

222. Many have the custom to announce each step with its name at the appropriate time.

223. There are two Torah mitzvos at the Seder - relating the story of *Yetzias Mitzrayim* and eating matza. (See nos. 150-154 for the required quantities of matza.)

224. There are three main Rabbinic mitzvos - drinking four cups of wine, eating *Maror*, and reciting Hallel.

225. Before commencing the Seder, the Seder plate with all the necessary items should be prepared and placed at the head of the table.

226. Additionally, one should bring a bowl of salt water, the wine and grape juice, and a cup and a Haggadah for each participant.

227. Women are obligated in all the mitzvos of the Seder since they too experienced the terrible slavery and miraculous redemption. In addition, the Jewish people were redeemed in the merit of the righteous women.

228. Children who have reached the age of *chinuch* (five or six) should try to fulfill all the mitzvos of the Seder. Since their obligation is Rabbinic, smaller quantities may be used for the mitzvos. The cup of grape juice (or wine)

must contain the minimum quantity of 86cc (approx. 3 fl. oz.), but it is sufficient for them to drink a cheekful.

229. For the three mitzvos of eating matza (*Hamotzi*, *Korech*, *Afikoman*) children can be given a small *kezayis* (10 grams), which should be eaten within nine minutes.

230. For each of the two mitzvos of eating *Maror* (*Maror* and *Korech*) children can be given a small *kezayis*, which should be eaten within nine minutes. If lettuce is used, one should take a leaf that measures 11" long and 4½" at the widest point.

231. Children aged five or six should be encouraged to remain at the Seder at least until the end of the meal and if possible until after the fourth cup of wine. It is for this reason that *Chazal* instituted many unusual procedures during the Seder to arouse the interest of the children and hold their attention during the evening. The Torah requires a father to relate the story of the slavery and of *Yetzias Mitzrayim* to his children, and the Haggadah emphasizes this by describing the four types of sons whom one may have to address. Some parents make the mistake of sending the children to bed after

reciting *Ma Nishtana* before they have heard the answers to their questions. It is advisable to see that the children sleep well on *erev Pesach* in order that they will have the strength and enthusiasm to remain awake during the Seder.

232. The father should bless the children before commencing the Seder as on Friday night. The night of Pesach is particularly appropriate for blessing the children since it was on this night that *Yaakov Avinu* received the blessings from his father *Yitzchak Avinu*.

For a boy:

יְשִׂמְךָ אֱלֹהִים כְּאֶפְרַיִם
וְכִמְנַשֶּׁה:

May God make you like Efrayim and Menashe.

May Hashem bless you and guard you.
May Hashem shine His countenance upon you and be gracious to you.
May Hashem turn His countenance to you and establish peace for you.

For a girl:

יְשִׂמֵךְ אֱלֹהִים כְּשָׂרָה רִבְקָה
רָחֵל וְלֵאָה:

May God make you like Sarah, Rivka, Rachel, and Leah.

יְבָרֶכְךָ יְהֹוָה וְיִשְׁמְרֶךָ:
יָאֵר יְהֹוָה פָּנָיו אֵלֶיךָ וִיחֻנֶּךָּ:
יִשָּׂא יְהֹוָה פָּנָיו אֵלֶיךָ
וְיָשֵׂם לְךָ שָׁלוֹם:

Kadesh

Recite Kiddush

233. The matzos should be covered during Kiddush. The rule throughout the Seder is that the matzos should be uncovered except when the wine is held. The reason is because matza is a more important food than wine, and it should be covered when special attention is given to the wine.

234. Some families have the custom that only the leader of the Seder recites Kiddush and the other participants fulfill the mitzvah by listening. Some have the custom that everyone recites Kiddush together, including the women and children.

235. All the participants should hold the wine during Kiddush whether they are listening or reciting it.

236. One may have any drinks other than wine and grape juice between Kiddush and *Urchatz*. Before Kiddush, one should have this in mind, and preferably place the drink on the table. The *b'racha Shehakol* should not be recited for the drink. If he did not have this drink in mind, he should restrict himself to water and recite the *b'racha Shehakol*.

237. Women who have the custom to listen to Kiddush and have already recited the *b'racha Shehecheyanu* when lighting candles should say 'amen' to that *b'racha* during Kiddush. The reason is because the *b'racha* recited when lighting candles refers only to the Yom Tov, whereas the *b'racha* recited during Kiddush refers also to all the mitzvos of the Seder.

238. Women who have the custom to recite Kiddush and have already recited the *b'racha Shehecheyanu* when lighting candles should not repeat that *b'racha* during Kiddush. Preferably, they should delay reciting the *b'racha Shehecheyanu* until during Kiddush.

239. Ideally, one should drink the entire cup even if it contains more than the required amount. If this is not possible, it is sufficient to drink the majority of the cup.

240. Ideally, one should drink the cup without pausing. If this is not possible, one may stop once for a short pause during the drinking. If this too is not possible, one fulfills his obligation if he drinks the required quantity within four minutes.

241. When the Seder is on *motzai Shabbos*, Kiddush and *Havdalah* are combined. For the *b'racha Borei Me'orei Ha'eish*, the common custom is to bring together two Yom Tov candles to make one flame. (This is not feasible when lighting with oil.) The *b'racha* for spices is not recited. If the family custom is to recite the Kiddush all together, the women should omit the third and fourth *brachos* (*Borei Me'orei Ha'eish* and *Hamavdil*) and listen to one of the men reciting them. According to some opinions, women may recite these *brachos*.

242. If a man forgot to recline, he should drink another cup immediately if he had in mind to do so. If he accidentally spoke, he should not repeat any *brachos* before drinking again. If he did not have in mind to drink another cup, he should not drink again.

243. A healthy person should not eat any food after Kiddush before the meal except for the *Karpas*. A sick or weak person may eat a small amount of food after Kiddush but not a vegetable. He should recite a *B'racha Acharona* before continuing with *Urchatz*. Children may eat any amount of food but not a vegetable.

244. Before Kiddush, one should have in mind to fulfill the mitzvah of Kiddush and the mitzvah of drinking the first of the four cups of wine.

245. One should have in mind that the *b'racha Borei Pri Hagafen* does not apply to the second cup of wine to be drunk before the meal.

246. One should have in mind that the *b'racha Shehecheyanu* applies to the Yom Tov and to all the mitzvos of the Seder.

247. Men should also have in mind that they would like to drink another cup if they forget to recline.

On Friday night begin here:

And there was evening and
there was morning –

The sixth day. And thus were completed
the heaven and the earth and all their
host. And by the seventh day God
completed his work that He had done,
and He ceased on the seventh day from
all His work that He had done. And God
blessed the seventh day and sanctified it,
because on it He abstained from all His
work that God created to make.

Quietly: וַיְהִי עֶרֶב וַיְהִי בֹקֶר:

יוֹם הַשִּׁשִּׁי: וַיְכֻלּוּ הַשָּׁמַיִם וְהָאָרֶץ
וְכָל צְבָאָם: וַיְכַל אֱלֹהִים בַּיּוֹם הַשְּׁבִיעִי
מְלַאכְתּוֹ אֲשֶׁר עָשָׂה, וַיִּשְׁבֹּת בַּיּוֹם
הַשְּׁבִיעִי מִכָּל מְלַאכְתּוֹ אֲשֶׁר עָשָׂה:
וַיְבָרֶךְ אֱלֹהִים אֶת יוֹם הַשְּׁבִיעִי וַיְקַדֵּשׁ
אֹתוֹ, כִּי בוֹ שָׁבַת מִכָּל מְלַאכְתּוֹ אֲשֶׁר
בָּרָא אֱלֹהִים לַעֲשׂוֹת:

On a weekday begin here (on Shabbos add the parenthetical phrases):

With your permission,
my masters, rabbis, and teachers;

Blessed are You, Hashem our God, King of the
universe, Who creates the fruit of the vine.

Blessed are You, Hashem our God, King of
the universe, Who has chosen us from every

סַבְרִי מָרָנָן וְרַבָּנָן וְרַבּוֹתַי

בָּרוּךְ אַתָּה יְיָ אֱלֹהֵינוּ מֶלֶךְ הָעוֹלָם, בּוֹרֵא
פְּרִי הַגָּפֶן:

בָּרוּךְ אַתָּה יְיָ אֱלֹהֵינוּ מֶלֶךְ הָעוֹלָם,
אֲשֶׁר בָּחַר בָּנוּ מִכָּל עָם, וְרוֹמְמָנוּ מִכָּל

nation, exalted us above every tongue, and sanctified us with His commandments. And You gave us, Hashem our God, with love (Sabbaths for rest and) seasons for happiness, festivals and times for joy, (this Shabbos and) this Festival of Matzos, the time of our freedom, (with love) a holy convocation, in remembrance of the Exodus from Egypt. For You have chosen us and sanctified us above all peoples, (and the Shabbos) and Your holy festivals (in love and favor) in happiness and joy You have granted us as a heritage. Blessed are You, Hashem, Who sanctifies (the Shabbos and) Yisroel and the festival seasons.

לָשׁוֹן, וְקִדְּשָׁנוּ בְּמִצְוֹתָיו, וַתִּתֶּן לָנוּ יְיָ אֱלֹהֵינוּ בְּאַהֲבָה (שַׁבָּתוֹת לִמְנוּחָה וּ)מוֹעֲדִים לְשִׂמְחָה, חַגִּים וּזְמַנִּים לְשָׂשׂוֹן (אֶת יוֹם הַשַּׁבָּת הַזֶּה וְ)אֶת יוֹם חַג הַמַּצּוֹת הַזֶּה זְמַן חֵרוּתֵנוּ (בְּאַהֲבָה) מִקְרָא קֹדֶשׁ, זֵכֶר לִיצִיאַת מִצְרָיִם. כִּי בָנוּ בָחַרְתָּ וְאוֹתָנוּ קִדַּשְׁתָּ מִכָּל הָעַמִּים, (וְשַׁבָּת) וּמוֹעֲדֵי קָדְשֶׁךָ (בְּאַהֲבָה וּבְרָצוֹן) בְּשִׂמְחָה וּבְשָׂשׂוֹן הִנְחַלְתָּנוּ. בָּרוּךְ אַתָּה יְיָ, מְקַדֵּשׁ (הַשַּׁבָּת וְ) יִשְׂרָאֵל וְהַזְּמַנִּים:

On motzai Shabbos add these two brachos:

Blessed are You, Hashem our God, King of the universe, Who creates the light of the fire.

בָּרוּךְ אַתָּה יְיָ אֱלֹהֵינוּ מֶלֶךְ הָעוֹלָם, בּוֹרֵא מְאוֹרֵי הָאֵשׁ:

Blessed are You, Hashem our God, King of the universe, Who distinguishes between holy and secular, between light and darkness, between Yisroel and the nations, between the seventh day and the six days of work. Between the sanctity of Shabbos and the sanctity of Yom Tov You have distinguished, and the seventh day from the six days of work You have sanctified. You have distinguished and sanctified Your people Yisroel with Your holiness. Blessed are You, Hashem, Who distinguishes between holiness and holiness.

בָּרוּךְ אַתָּה יְיָ אֱלֹהֵינוּ מֶלֶךְ הָעוֹלָם, הַמַּבְדִּיל בֵּין קֹדֶשׁ לְחוֹל, בֵּין אוֹר לְחשֶׁךְ, בֵּין יִשְׂרָאֵל לָעַמִּים, בֵּין יוֹם הַשְּׁבִיעִי לְשֵׁשֶׁת יְמֵי הַמַּעֲשֶׂה, בֵּין קְדֻשַּׁת שַׁבָּת לִקְדֻשַּׁת יוֹם טוֹב הִבְדַּלְתָּ, וְאֶת יוֹם הַשְּׁבִיעִי מִשֵּׁשֶׁת יְמֵי הַמַּעֲשֶׂה קִדַּשְׁתָּ, הִבְדַּלְתָּ וְקִדַּשְׁתָּ אֶת עַמְּךָ יִשְׂרָאֵל בִּקְדֻשָּׁתֶךָ: בָּרוּךְ אַתָּה יְיָ, הַמַּבְדִּיל בֵּין קֹדֶשׁ לְקֹדֶשׁ:

On all nights continue here:

Blessed are You, Hashem our God, King of the universe, Who has kept us alive, sustained us, and brought us to this season.

בָּרוּךְ אַתָּה יְיָ אֱלֹהֵינוּ מֶלֶךְ הָעוֹלָם, שֶׁהֶחֱיָנוּ וְקִיְּמָנוּ וְהִגִּיעָנוּ לַזְּמַן הַזֶּה:

Men must recline when drinking the wine.

Urchatz

Wash the hands

248. Although the meal has not yet been served, the hands must be washed before eating the *Karpas*. The reason is because one is required to wash hands without a *b'racha* before eating a wet food. Some people are lenient about this throughout the year and rely on the opinions that this was necessary only in the time of the *Beis Hamikdash*. On the Seder night everyone is particular to fulfill this mitzvah since it is a time of extreme holiness. In addition, the children will notice something unusual and will be aroused to ask questions.

249. All the participants should wash their hands. In some families, only the leader of the Seder washes his hands. Some have the custom that the leader of the Seder has his hands washed by one of the children in order to show freedom and royalty.

250. When washing, all the rules regarding washing for bread apply (e.g. removal of rings) except that a *b'racha* is not recited.

251. A person who mistakenly recited the *b'racha* on the washing of the hands should eat a *kezayis* of *Karpas*. Even though this quantity is eaten, a *B'racha Acharona* should not be recited.

252. Care should be taken not to speak after the washing until the *Karpas* is eaten unless the talking is connected to the performance of the mitzvah.

The hands are washed but a b'racha is not recited.

כַּרְפַּס
Karpas
Eat the vegetable

253. We eat *Karpas* in order to stimulate the children to ask questions since it is unusual to eat vegetables before the meal. The letters of the word *Karpas* (כרפס) when reversed read ס' פרך, alluding to the 600,000 Jews (ס') who toiled in hard labor (פרך).

254. The *Karpas* is dipped in salt water to stimulate the children to ask questions when seeing something unusual. Another reason is in order to demonstrate our freedom since it is the manner of royalty to eat their food in this way.

255. There is no standard custom as to who dips the *Karpas*. Some find it convenient for the leader of the Seder to dip several pieces of *Karpas* into salt water before distributing them.

256. Each person should be given a piece of *Karpas* less than a *kezayis*, i.e. less than 30cc.

257. The *Karpas* should be held with one's fingers since according to some opinions there would be no requirement to wash one's hands when eating with a fork. This is particularly important for those who use potato for *Karpas*.

258. The main custom is for each person to recite his own *b'racha*.

259. The remaining *Karpas* may be removed, but some have the custom to leave a piece of *Karpas* on the Seder plate until the meal. The salt water may be removed.

Dip less than a kezayis of Karpas in salt water and have in mind that the b'racha Borei P'ri Ha'adama should include the Maror that will be eaten later in the Seder. The prevalent custom is to eat the Karpas without reclining.

Blessed are You, Hashem our God, King of the universe, Who creates the fruit of the ground.

בָּרוּךְ אַתָּה יְיָ אֱלֹהֵינוּ מֶלֶךְ הָעוֹלָם, בּוֹרֵא פְּרִי הָאֲדָמָה:

יחץ

Yachatz

Break the middle matza

260. The middle matza is broken because the Torah refers to matza as 'the bread of the poor' (*Devarim* 16:3), and a poor man, being unable to afford a whole loaf, usually eats pieces of bread. The middle matza is chosen since the second *b'racha* recited on the matza (*Al Achilas Matza*) refers specifically to this second matza.

261. The smaller piece is returned to the Seder plate and the larger one is wrapped up in a cloth and put aside to use as *Afikoman*. The smaller piece should be at least a *kezayis*. There is a custom for the children to take the *Afikoman* and hide it when the leader of the Seder is not watching. This is to encourage the children to remain awake until the end of the meal when the *Afikoman* is eaten.

262. Since the piece for *Afikoman* is not usually sufficient for all the participants, extra pieces of matza should be prepared specifically for the *Afikoman*.

מַגִּיד

Maggid

Relate the story of the Haggadah

263. Before beginning the narrative of the Haggadah, everyone should have in mind to fulfill the Torah obligation to relate the story of *Yetzias Mitzrayim*.

264. The mitzvah is fulfilled by discussing three basic themes:

    (i) The wickedness of the Egyptians and the excruciating persecutions that they afflicted upon the Jewish people during the long years of slavery.

    (ii) The miraculous plagues that Hashem brought upon the Egyptians and the punishments meted out to them measure for measure.

    (iii) Expressing our thanks and praise to Hashem for the wonderful acts of kindness that He performed for the Jewish people by redeeming them from bondage and choosing them as His special nation. All these aspects are elaborated upon during the recital of the Haggadah.

265. One does not fulfill the mitzvah by mere recital of the Haggadah if he does not understand the words. Those who are not familiar with Hebrew are strongly advised to spend time before Pesach studying the Haggadah in order that the Seder night will be a deep and more meaningful experience. It is a tragedy that so many people expend vast amounts of time and energy in preparing the house for Pesach but are unable to find meaning and joy at the Seder. In any event, the leader of the Seder must ensure that everyone understands at least the most essential sections of the narrative.

266. The most essential sections of the narrative are the ten plagues and from the section that begins 'Rabban Gamliel used to say' until the second cup is drunk.

267. It is acceptable either to recite the Haggadah or to just listen, as long as one understands what is being said. Most people follow the custom to recite the Haggadah if they are fluent in Hebrew.

268. When saying 'Ha Lachma Anya', the leader of the Seder should hold the broken middle matza and show it to everyone. Some have the custom to hold all three matzos.

This is the bread of affliction that our fathers ate in the land of Egypt. Whoever is hungry, let him come and eat. Whoever is needy, let him come to our Pesach meal. This year we are here, next year may we be in *Eretz Yisroel*. This year we are slaves, next year may we be free men.

הָא לַחְמָא עַנְיָא דִּי אֲכַלוּ אֲבָהָתַנָא בְּאַרְעָא דְמִצְרָיִם. כָּל דִּכְפִין יֵיתֵי וְיֵכוֹל. כָּל דִּצְרִיךְ יֵיתֵי וְיִפְסַח. הָשַׁתָּא הָכָא, לְשָׁנָה הַבָּאָה בְּאַרְעָא דְיִשְׂרָאֵל. הָשַׁתָּא עַבְדֵי, לְשָׁנָה הַבָּאָה בְּנֵי חוֹרִין:

The matzos should be removed from the table or at least moved away from the leader of the Seder.

269. The matzos are moved away at this point to arouse the interest of the children to ask why the food has been removed before eating any of it. The father should reply that we may not eat the meal until we relate the story of *Yetzias Mitzrayim*.

270. The second cup of wine is filled.

271. From this point until the second cup is drunk, it is preferable not to have any food or drink. Children may eat and drink freely.

272. The custom is for the youngest child capable of asking the questions to recite *Ma Nishtana*. If the child is hesitant, his father may assist him. If there are no children present, one of the participants should ask the four questions.

273. It is unnecessary for everyone to repeat *Ma Nishtana* before continuing the Haggadah, but some have the custom to do so.

Why is this night different from all other nights?

On all other nights we may eat chametz and matza; this night, only matza.

On all other nights we may eat all kinds of vegetables; this night, bitter herbs.

On all other nights we do not dip even once; this night, twice.

On all other nights we eat sitting or reclining; this night, we all recline.

מַה נִּשְׁתַּנָּה הַלַּיְלָה הַזֶּה מִכָּל הַלֵּילוֹת:

שֶׁבְּכָל הַלֵּילוֹת אָנוּ אוֹכְלִין חָמֵץ וּמַצָּה, הַלַּיְלָה הַזֶּה כֻּלּוֹ מַצָּה:

שֶׁבְּכָל הַלֵּילוֹת אָנוּ אוֹכְלִין שְׁאָר יְרָקוֹת, הַלַּיְלָה הַזֶּה מָרוֹר:

שֶׁבְּכָל הַלֵּילוֹת אֵין אָנוּ מַטְבִּילִין אֲפִלוּ פַּעַם אֶחָת, הַלַּיְלָה הַזֶּה שְׁתֵּי פְעָמִים:

שֶׁבְּכָל הַלֵּילוֹת אָנוּ אוֹכְלִין בֵּין יוֹשְׁבִין וּבֵין מְסוּבִּין, הַלַּיְלָה הַזֶּה כֻּלָּנוּ מְסוּבִּין:

The matzos should be returned to their place in front of the leader of the Seder and left uncovered during the narrative. The story of Yetzias Mitzrayim is now related in detail.

274. For most people it is sufficient to recite the standard text of the Haggadah pausing occasionally to elaborate on the essential sections. Analyses of the text are out of place, rather a person should quote Midrashim and commentaries that describe the slavery and the miracles. It is important to explain the story to the participants according to the level of their understanding. In particular, one should try to hold the attention of the children during the narrative by describing the story as vividly as possible.

275. One should keep an eye on the time since every effort must be made to eat the *Afikoman* before *halachic* midnight. As a rough guide, one should complete the narrative of the Haggadah and drink the second cup of wine approximately two hours before *halachic* midnight. If there is time to spare, one should expound on the story during the meal.

276. Although some parts of the story do not seem to apply to a convert (e.g. we were slaves etc.), he should say the entire narrative.

277. During the narrative, one should sit upright with awe and respect.

We were slaves to Pharaoh in Egypt, and Hashem our God took us out from there with a strong hand and an outstretched arm. And if the Holy One, blessed is He, had not taken our fathers out of Egypt, then we, our children, and our children's children would still be enslaved to Pharaoh in Egypt.

עֲבָדִים הָיִינוּ לְפַרְעֹה בְּמִצְרַיִם, וַיּוֹצִיאֵנוּ יְיָ אֱלֹהֵינוּ מִשָּׁם בְּיָד חֲזָקָה וּבִזְרוֹעַ נְטוּיָה. וְאִלּוּ לֹא הוֹצִיא הַקָּדוֹשׁ בָּרוּךְ הוּא אֶת אֲבוֹתֵינוּ מִמִּצְרַיִם, הֲרֵי אָנוּ וּבָנֵינוּ וּבְנֵי בָנֵינוּ מְשֻׁעְבָּדִים הָיִינוּ לְפַרְעֹה בְּמִצְרָיִם:

The Guidelines Haggadah

And even if we were all men of wisdom, understanding, experience, and knowledge of the Torah, it would be a mitzvah for us to recount the story of the Exodus from Egypt. Whoever elaborates on the story of the Exodus is praiseworthy.

It once happened that Rabbi Eliezer, Rabbi Yehoshua, Rabbi Elazar ben Azaryah, Rabbi Akiva, and Rabbi Tarfon were reclining (at the Seder) in B'nei B'rak. They discussed the Exodus the entire night until their students came and told them, "Our teachers, the time has arrived to recite the morning Shema".

וַאֲפִלּוּ כֻּלָּנוּ חֲכָמִים, כֻּלָּנוּ נְבוֹנִים, כֻּלָּנוּ זְקֵנִים, כֻּלָּנוּ יוֹדְעִים אֶת הַתּוֹרָה, מִצְוָה עָלֵינוּ לְסַפֵּר בִּיצִיאַת מִצְרָיִם. וְכָל הַמַּרְבֶּה לְסַפֵּר בִּיצִיאַת מִצְרַיִם, הֲרֵי זֶה מְשֻׁבָּח:

מַעֲשֶׂה בְּרַבִּי אֱלִיעֶזֶר וְרַבִּי יְהוֹשֻׁעַ וְרַבִּי אֶלְעָזָר בֶּן עֲזַרְיָה וְרַבִּי עֲקִיבָא וְרַבִּי טַרְפוֹן שֶׁהָיוּ מְסוּבִּין בִּבְנֵי בְרַק, וְהָיוּ מְסַפְּרִים בִּיצִיאַת מִצְרַיִם כָּל אוֹתוֹ הַלַּיְלָה, עַד שֶׁבָּאוּ תַלְמִידֵיהֶם וְאָמְרוּ לָהֶם, רַבּוֹתֵינוּ הִגִּיעַ זְמַן קְרִיאַת שְׁמַע שֶׁל שַׁחֲרִית:

Rabbi Elazar ben Azaryah said, "I am like a seventy year old man and I could not succeed in proving that the Exodus should be mentioned every night until Ben Zoma explained it". The Torah says, "So that you will remember the day that you left the land of Egypt all the days of your life" (Devarim 16:3). "The days of your life" refers to the daytime; "all the days of your life" refers to the nights. The Rabbis say, "The days of your life" refers to this world; "all the days of your life" includes the days of Mashiach.

Blessed is the Omnipresent, Blessed is He. Blessed is the One Who has given the Torah to His people Yisroel. Blessed is He.

The Torah speaks about four sons: one wise, one wicked, one simple, and one who does not know how to ask.

אָמַר רַבִּי אֶלְעָזָר בֶּן עֲזַרְיָה הֲרֵי אֲנִי כְּבֶן שִׁבְעִים שָׁנָה, וְלֹא זָכִיתִי שֶׁתֵּאָמֵר יְצִיאַת מִצְרַיִם בַּלֵּילוֹת עַד שֶׁדְּרָשָׁהּ בֶּן זוֹמָא, שֶׁנֶּאֱמַר לְמַעַן תִּזְכֹּר אֶת יוֹם צֵאתְךָ מֵאֶרֶץ מִצְרַיִם כֹּל יְמֵי חַיֶּיךָ. יְמֵי חַיֶּיךָ הַיָּמִים, כֹּל יְמֵי חַיֶּיךָ הַלֵּילוֹת. וַחֲכָמִים אוֹמְרִים יְמֵי חַיֶּיךָ הָעוֹלָם הַזֶּה, כֹּל יְמֵי חַיֶּיךָ לְהָבִיא לִימוֹת הַמָּשִׁיחַ:

בָּרוּךְ הַמָּקוֹם, בָּרוּךְ הוּא. בָּרוּךְ שֶׁנָּתַן תּוֹרָה לְעַמּוֹ יִשְׂרָאֵל, בָּרוּךְ הוּא:

כְּנֶגֶד אַרְבָּעָה בָנִים דִּבְּרָה תוֹרָה: אֶחָד חָכָם, וְאֶחָד רָשָׁע, וְאֶחָד תָּם, וְאֶחָד שֶׁאֵינוֹ יוֹדֵעַ לִשְׁאֹל:

What does the wise son say?
"What are the testimonies, statutes, and ordinances that Hashem our God has commanded you?" (Devarim 6:20). Therefore, tell him the laws of the Pesach offering: that one may not eat dessert after eating the Pesach offering.

What does the wicked son say? "What is this service to you?" (Shemos 12:26). "To you", but not to him. Since he has excluded himself from the community, he has denied the essentials of our faith. Therefore, blunt his teeth and say to him, "It is because of this (service) that Hashem acted for me when I went out of Egypt." (Shemos 13:8). "For me", but not for him. Had he been there, he would not have been redeemed.

What does the simple son say?
"What is this?". "And you shall say to him, 'Hashem took us out of Egypt, the house of slaves, with a strong hand.'" (Shemos 13:14).

חָכָם מָה הוּא אוֹמֵר: מָה הָעֵדֹת וְהַחֻקִּים וְהַמִּשְׁפָּטִים אֲשֶׁר צִוָּה יְהֹוָה אֱלֹהֵינוּ אֶתְכֶם. וְאַף אַתָּה אֱמָר לוֹ כְּהִלְכוֹת הַפֶּסַח, אֵין מַפְטִירִין אַחַר הַפֶּסַח אֲפִיקוֹמָן:

רָשָׁע מָה הוּא אוֹמֵר: מָה הָעֲבֹדָה הַזֹּאת לָכֶם. לָכֶם וְלֹא לוֹ. וּלְפִי שֶׁהוֹצִיא אֶת עַצְמוֹ מִן הַכְּלָל כָּפַר בְּעִקָּר, וְאַף אַתָּה הַקְהֵה אֶת שִׁנָּיו וֶאֱמָר לוֹ, בַּעֲבוּר זֶה עָשָׂה יְהֹוָה לִי בְּצֵאתִי מִמִּצְרָיִם: לִי וְלֹא לוֹ. אִלּוּ הָיָה שָׁם לֹא הָיָה נִגְאָל:

תָּם מָה הוּא אוֹמֵר: מַה זֹּאת. וְאָמַרְתָּ אֵלָיו בְּחֹזֶק יָד הוֹצִיאָנוּ יְהֹוָה מִמִּצְרַיִם מִבֵּית עֲבָדִים:

And as for the son who does not know to ask, you must initiate the discussion with him, as it says, "And you shall tell your son on that day, saying, 'It is because of this (service) that Hashem acted for me when I went out of Egypt.'" (Shemos 13:8).

One might think that the obligation to relate the story of the Exodus begins on the first of Nissan, but the Torah states, "On that day". "On that day" might be understood to mean during the daytime (of erev Pesach); therefore the Torah says, "Because of this". I cannot say "because of this" except when matza and Maror are placed in front of you.

וְשֶׁאֵינוֹ יוֹדֵעַ לִשְׁאֹל אַתְּ פְּתַח לוֹ, שֶׁנֶּאֱמַר, וְהִגַּדְתָּ לְבִנְךָ בַּיּוֹם הַהוּא לֵאמֹר בַּעֲבוּר זֶה עָשָׂה יְהֹוָה לִי בְּצֵאתִי מִמִּצְרָיִם:

יָכוֹל מֵרֹאשׁ חֹדֶשׁ, תַּלְמוּד לוֹמַר בַּיּוֹם הַהוּא. אִי בַּיּוֹם הַהוּא יָכוֹל מִבְּעוֹד יוֹם, תַּלְמוּד לוֹמַר בַּעֲבוּר זֶה. בַּעֲבוּר זֶה לֹא אָמַרְתִּי אֶלָּא בְּשָׁעָה שֶׁיֵּשׁ מַצָּה וּמָרוֹר מוּנָחִים לְפָנֶיךָ:

At first, our ancestors were idol worshippers, but now the Omnipresent has brought us close, to serve Him. As it says, "And Yehoshua said to all the people, "Thus says Hashem, the God of Yisroel; Your fathers always lived beyond the [Euphrates] river, Terach the father of Avraham and Nachor, and they served other gods. Then I took your father Avraham from beyond the river and led him through all the land of Canaan. And I multiplied his offspring and gave him Yitzchak, and to Yitzchak I gave Yaakov and Eisav, and to Eisav I gave Mount Seir as an inheritance, and Yaakov and his children went down to Egypt.'" (Yehoshua 24:2-4).

מִתְּחִלָּה עוֹבְדֵי עֲבוֹדָה זָרָה הָיוּ אֲבוֹתֵינוּ, וְעַכְשָׁיו קֵרְבָנוּ הַמָּקוֹם לַעֲבוֹדָתוֹ, שֶׁנֶּאֱמַר, וַיֹּאמֶר יְהוֹשֻׁעַ אֶל כָּל הָעָם כֹּה אָמַר יְהוָֹה אֱלֹהֵי יִשְׂרָאֵל בְּעֵבֶר הַנָּהָר יָשְׁבוּ אֲבוֹתֵיכֶם מֵעוֹלָם, תֶּרַח אֲבִי אַבְרָהָם וַאֲבִי נָחוֹר, וַיַּעַבְדוּ אֱלֹהִים אֲחֵרִים: וָאֶקַּח אֶת אֲבִיכֶם אֶת אַבְרָהָם מֵעֵבֶר הַנָּהָר, וָאוֹלֵךְ אוֹתוֹ בְּכָל אֶרֶץ כְּנָעַן, וָאַרְבֶּה אֶת זַרְעוֹ, וָאֶתֶּן לוֹ אֶת יִצְחָק: וָאֶתֵּן לְיִצְחָק אֶת יַעֲקֹב וְאֶת עֵשָׂו, וָאֶתֵּן לְעֵשָׂו אֶת הַר שֵׂעִיר לָרֶשֶׁת אוֹתוֹ, וְיַעֲקֹב וּבָנָיו יָרְדוּ מִצְרָיִם:

Blessed is He Who keeps His promise to Yisroel; blessed is He. For the Holy One, blessed is He, calculated the end [of our exile] in order to fulfill what He had said to our father Avraham at the *Bris Bein Habesarim*. As it says, "And He said to Avram, 'Know for sure that your offspring shall be strangers in a land that is not theirs, and they will enslave and oppress them for four hundred years. But I will also execute judgment on the nation that enslaves them and afterwards they will leave with great possessions'" (Bereishis 15:13-14).

בָּרוּךְ שׁוֹמֵר הַבְטָחָתוֹ לְיִשְׂרָאֵל, בָּרוּךְ הוּא. שֶׁהַקָּדוֹשׁ בָּרוּךְ הוּא חִשַּׁב אֶת הַקֵּץ, לַעֲשׂוֹת כְּמָה שֶׁאָמַר לְאַבְרָהָם אָבִינוּ בִּבְרִית בֵּין הַבְּתָרִים, שֶׁנֶּאֱמַר, וַיֹּאמֶר לְאַבְרָם יָדֹעַ תֵּדַע כִּי גֵר יִהְיֶה זַרְעֲךָ בְּאֶרֶץ לֹא לָהֶם וַעֲבָדוּם וְעִנּוּ אֹתָם אַרְבַּע מֵאוֹת שָׁנָה: וְגַם אֶת הַגּוֹי אֲשֶׁר יַעֲבֹדוּ דָּן אָנֹכִי, וְאַחֲרֵי כֵן יֵצְאוּ בִּרְכֻשׁ גָּדוֹל:

The Guidelines Haggadah   72

Cover the matzos.
Everyone should hold the cup of wine.

And this is what has stood by our fathers and us. Because not just one has risen against us to destroy us, but in every generation they rise against us to destroy us. But the Holy One, blessed is He, rescues us from their hand.

וְהִיא שֶׁעָמְדָה לַאֲבוֹתֵינוּ וְלָנוּ, שֶׁלֹּא אֶחָד בִּלְבָד עָמַד עָלֵינוּ לְכַלּוֹתֵינוּ, אֶלָּא שֶׁבְּכָל דּוֹר וָדוֹר עוֹמְדִים עָלֵינוּ לְכַלּוֹתֵינוּ, וְהַקָּדוֹשׁ בָּרוּךְ הוּא מַצִּילֵנוּ מִיָּדָם:

Put down the wine and uncover the matzos.

Go and learn what Lavan the Aramean attempted to do to Yaakov Avinu. For Pharaoh decreed only against the male children, while Lavan attempted to uproot everything, as it says, "An Aramean attempted to destroy my father. And he went down to Egypt and sojourned there with few people, and there he became a great, mighty, and numerous nation" (Devarim 26:5).

צֵא וּלְמַד מַה בִּקֵּשׁ לָבָן הָאֲרַמִּי לַעֲשׂוֹת לְיַעֲקֹב אָבִינוּ, שֶׁפַּרְעֹה לֹא גָזַר אֶלָּא עַל הַזְּכָרִים, וְלָבָן בִּקֵּשׁ לַעֲקוֹר אֶת הַכֹּל, שֶׁנֶּאֱמַר, אֲרַמִּי אֹבֵד אָבִי וַיֵּרֶד מִצְרַיְמָה וַיָּגָר שָׁם בִּמְתֵי מְעָט, וַיְהִי שָׁם לְגוֹי גָּדוֹל עָצוּם וָרָב:

And he went down to Egypt - compelled by Divine decree.

וַיֵּרֶד מִצְרַיְמָה, אָנוּס עַל פִּי הַדִּבּוּר:

And sojourned there - this teaches that Yaakov Avinu did not go down to Egypt to settle there, but only to stay there temporarily, as it says, "And they [the sons of Yaakov] said to Pharaoh, 'We have come to sojourn in the land since there is no pasture for your servants' flocks, because the famine is severe in the land of Canaan. So now, please let your servants dwell in the land of Goshen'" (Bereishis 47:4).

וַיָּגָר שָׁם, מְלַמֵּד שֶׁלֹּא יָרַד יַעֲקֹב אָבִינוּ לְהִשְׁתַּקֵּעַ בְּמִצְרַיִם אֶלָּא לָגוּר שָׁם, שֶׁנֶּאֱמַר, וַיֹּאמְרוּ אֶל פַּרְעֹה לָגוּר בָּאָרֶץ בָּאנוּ, כִּי אֵין מִרְעֶה לַצֹּאן אֲשֶׁר לַעֲבָדֶיךָ, כִּי כָבֵד הָרָעָב בְּאֶרֶץ כְּנָעַן, וְעַתָּה יֵשְׁבוּ נָא עֲבָדֶיךָ בְּאֶרֶץ גֹּשֶׁן:

With few people - as it says, "With seventy souls your forefathers went down to Egypt, and now Hashem your God has made you as numerous as the stars of the heaven" (Devarim 10:22).

בִּמְתֵי מְעָט, כְּמָה שֶׁנֶּאֱמַר, בְּשִׁבְעִים נֶפֶשׁ יָרְדוּ אֲבֹתֶיךָ מִצְרָיְמָה, וְעַתָּה שָׂמְךָ יְהֹוָה אֱלֹהֶיךָ כְּכוֹכְבֵי הַשָּׁמַיִם לָרֹב:

The Guidelines Haggadah

And there he became a great nation - this teaches that the people of Yisroel were distinctive there.

Great and Mighty - as it says, "And the children of Yisroel were fruitful and increased abundantly and multiplied and became exceedingly mighty. And the land was filled with them" (Shemos 1:7).

Numerous - as it says, "I made you as numerous as the plants of the field. You multiplied and grew, developed outstanding beauty and maturity, your hair had grown, but you were naked and bare. And I passed over you and saw you wallowing in your blood, and I said to you, 'Through your blood you shall live', and I said to you, 'Through your blood you shall live'" (Yechezkel 16:7-6).

וַיְהִי שָׁם לְגוֹי, מְלַמֵּד שֶׁהָיוּ יִשְׂרָאֵל מְצֻיָּנִים שָׁם:

גָּדוֹל עָצוּם, כְּמָה שֶׁנֶּאֱמַר, וּבְנֵי יִשְׂרָאֵל פָּרוּ וַיִּשְׁרְצוּ וַיִּרְבּוּ וַיַּעַצְמוּ בִּמְאֹד מְאֹד וַתִּמָּלֵא הָאָרֶץ אֹתָם:

וָרָב, כְּמָה שֶׁנֶּאֱמַר, רְבָבָה כְּצֶמַח הַשָּׂדֶה נְתַתִּיךְ, וַתִּרְבִּי וַתִּגְדְּלִי וַתָּבֹאִי בַּעֲדִי עֲדָיִים, שָׁדַיִם נָכֹנוּ וּשְׂעָרֵךְ צִמֵּחַ וְאַתְּ עֵרֹם וְעֶרְיָה: וָאֶעֱבֹר עָלַיִךְ וָאֶרְאֵךְ מִתְבּוֹסֶסֶת בְּדָמָיִךְ, וָאֹמַר לָךְ בְּדָמַיִךְ חֲיִי, וָאֹמַר לָךְ בְּדָמַיִךְ חֲיִי:

And the Egyptians did evil to us, and afflicted us, and imposed hard labor upon us (*Devarim* 26:6).

And the Egyptians did evil to us - as it says, "Let us deal wisely with them lest they multiply, and should a war come, they may join our enemies and fight against us and leave the country" (*Shemos* 1:10).

And afflicted us - as it says, "And they put task masters over them in order to afflict them with their burdens, and they built storage cities for Pharoah - Pisom and Ra'amses" (*Shemos* 1:11).

And imposed hard labor upon us - as it says, "And the Egyptians enslaved the children of Yisroel with crushing labor" (*Shemos* 1:13).

וַיָּרֵעוּ אֹתָנוּ הַמִּצְרִים וַיְעַנּוּנוּ, וַיִּתְּנוּ עָלֵינוּ עֲבֹדָה קָשָׁה:

וַיָּרֵעוּ אֹתָנוּ הַמִּצְרִים, כְּמָה שֶׁנֶּאֱמַר, הָבָה נִתְחַכְּמָה לוֹ פֶּן יִרְבֶּה וְהָיָה כִּי תִקְרֶאנָה מִלְחָמָה וְנוֹסַף גַּם הוּא עַל שֹׂנְאֵינוּ וְנִלְחַם בָּנוּ וְעָלָה מִן הָאָרֶץ:

וַיְעַנּוּנוּ, כְּמָה שֶׁנֶּאֱמַר, וַיָּשִׂימוּ עָלָיו שָׂרֵי מִסִּים לְמַעַן עַנֹּתוֹ בְּסִבְלֹתָם, וַיִּבֶן עָרֵי מִסְכְּנוֹת לְפַרְעֹה אֶת פִּתֹם וְאֶת רַעַמְסֵס:

וַיִּתְּנוּ עָלֵינוּ עֲבֹדָה קָשָׁה, כְּמָה שֶׁנֶּאֱמַר, וַיַּעֲבִדוּ מִצְרַיִם אֶת בְּנֵי יִשְׂרָאֵל בְּפָרֶךְ:

And we cried out to Hashem the God of our fathers, and Hashem heard our voice and saw our affliction, our misery, and our oppression (*Devarim* 26:7).

And we cried out to Hashem the God of our fathers - as it says, "And it happened during those many days that the king of Egypt died, and the children of Yisroel groaned from the slavery and cried. And their cry from the work rose up to God" (*Shemos* 2:23).

And Hashem heard our voice - as it says, "And God heard their groaning and God remembered His covenant with Avraham, with Yitzchak, and with Yaakov" (*Shemos* 2:24).

וַנִּצְעַק אֶל יְהֹוָה אֱלֹהֵי אֲבֹתֵינוּ וַיִּשְׁמַע יְהֹוָה אֶת קֹלֵנוּ וַיַּרְא אֶת עָנְיֵנוּ וְאֶת עֲמָלֵנוּ וְאֶת לַחֲצֵנוּ:

וַנִּצְעַק אֶל יְהֹוָה אֱלֹהֵי אֲבֹתֵינוּ, כְּמָה שֶׁנֶּאֱמַר, וַיְהִי בַיָּמִים הָרַבִּים הָהֵם וַיָּמָת מֶלֶךְ מִצְרַיִם וַיֵּאָנְחוּ בְנֵי יִשְׂרָאֵל מִן הָעֲבֹדָה וַיִּזְעָקוּ, וַתַּעַל שַׁוְעָתָם אֶל הָאֱלֹהִים מִן הָעֲבֹדָה:

וַיִּשְׁמַע יְהֹוָה אֶת קֹלֵנוּ, כְּמָה שֶׁנֶּאֱמַר, וַיִּשְׁמַע אֱלֹהִים אֶת נַאֲקָתָם, וַיִּזְכֹּר אֱלֹהִים אֶת בְּרִיתוֹ אֶת אַבְרָהָם אֶת יִצְחָק וְאֶת יַעֲקֹב:

And saw our affliction - this refers to the disruption of family life, as it says, "And God saw the children of Yisroel, and God took note of it" (*Shemos 2:25*).

And our misery - this refers to the children, as it says, "Every newborn son you shall cast into the river, and every daughter you shall let live" (*Shemos 1:22*).

And our oppression - this refers to the pressure, as it says, "And I have also seen how the Egyptians are oppressing them" (*Shemos 3:9*).

And Hashem brought us out from Egypt with a mighty hand and an outstretched arm, with great awe, with signs and with wonders (*Devarim 26:8*).

וַיַּרְא אֶת עָנְיֵנוּ, זוֹ פְּרִישׁוּת דֶּרֶךְ אֶרֶץ, כְּמָה שֶׁנֶּאֱמַר, וַיַּרְא אֱלֹהִים אֶת בְּנֵי יִשְׂרָאֵל וַיֵּדַע אֱלֹהִים:

וְאֶת עֲמָלֵנוּ, אֵלּוּ הַבָּנִים, כְּמָה שֶׁנֶּאֱמַר, כָּל הַבֵּן הַיִּלּוֹד הַיְאֹרָה תַּשְׁלִיכֻהוּ וְכָל הַבַּת תְּחַיּוּן:

וְאֶת לַחֲצֵנוּ, זוֹ הַדְּחַק, כְּמָה שֶׁנֶּאֱמַר, וְגַם רָאִיתִי אֶת הַלַּחַץ אֲשֶׁר מִצְרַיִם לֹחֲצִים אֹתָם:

וַיּוֹצִאֵנוּ יְהֹוָה מִמִּצְרַיִם בְּיָד חֲזָקָה וּבִזְרֹעַ נְטוּיָה וּבְמֹרָא גָּדֹל וּבְאֹתוֹת וּבְמֹפְתִים:

The Guidelines Haggadah

And Hashem brought us out from Egypt - not through an angel, not through a Seraph, and not through a messenger, but the Holy one, blessed is He, Himself in His glory, as it says, "And I will pass through the land of Egypt on that night, and I will slay every firstborn in the land of Egypt from man to beast, and upon all the gods of Egypt I will execute judgments, I Hashem" (Shemos 12:12).

And I will pass through the land of Egypt on that night - I and not an angel. And I will slay every firstborn in the land of Egypt - I and not a Seraph. And upon all the gods of Egypt I will execute judgments - I and not a messenger.

I Hashem - it is I and no other.

וַיּוֹצִאֵנוּ יְהֹוָה מִמִּצְרַיִם, לֹא עַל יְדֵי מַלְאָךְ וְלֹא עַל יְדֵי שָׂרָף וְלֹא עַל יְדֵי שָׁלִיחַ, אֶלָּא הַקָּדוֹשׁ בָּרוּךְ הוּא בִּכְבוֹדוֹ וּבְעַצְמוֹ, שֶׁנֶּאֱמַר, וְעָבַרְתִּי בְאֶרֶץ מִצְרַיִם בַּלַּיְלָה הַזֶּה, וְהִכֵּיתִי כָל בְּכוֹר בְּאֶרֶץ מִצְרַיִם מֵאָדָם וְעַד בְּהֵמָה וּבְכָל אֱלֹהֵי מִצְרַיִם אֶעֱשֶׂה שְׁפָטִים אֲנִי יְהֹוָה:

וְעָבַרְתִּי בְאֶרֶץ מִצְרַיִם בַּלַּיְלָה הַזֶּה, אֲנִי וְלֹא מַלְאָךְ: וְהִכֵּיתִי כָל בְּכוֹר בְּאֶרֶץ מִצְרַיִם, אֲנִי וְלֹא שָׂרָף: וּבְכָל אֱלֹהֵי מִצְרַיִם אֶעֱשֶׂה שְׁפָטִים, אֲנִי וְלֹא הַשָּׁלִיחַ:

אֲנִי יְהֹוָה, אֲנִי הוּא וְלֹא אַחֵר:

With a mighty hand - this refers to the pestilence, as it says, "Behold the hand of Hashem shall strike your herds in the field; the horses, the donkeys, the camels, the cattle, and the sheep; a very severe pestilence" (*Shemos* 9:3).

With an outstretched arm - this refers to the sword, as it says, "And His drawn sword in His hand, outstretched over Yerushalayim" (*Divrei Hayamim* I 21:16).

With great awe - this refers to the revelation of the Shechina, as it says, "Or has God ever before come to extract one nation from the midst of another nation; with challenges, with signs, with wonders, by war, and with a mighty hand and outstretched arm, and with great awe, like Hashem your God did for you in Egypt, before your eyes?" (*Devarim* 4:34).

בְּיָד חֲזָקָה, זוֹ הַדֶּבֶר, כְּמָה שֶׁנֶּאֱמַר, הִנֵּה יַד יְהֹוָה הוֹיָה בְּמִקְנְךָ אֲשֶׁר בַּשָּׂדֶה בַּסּוּסִים בַּחֲמֹרִים בַּגְּמַלִּים בַּבָּקָר וּבַצֹּאן, דֶּבֶר כָּבֵד מְאֹד:

וּבִזְרֹעַ נְטוּיָה, זוֹ הַחֶרֶב, כְּמָה שֶׁנֶּאֱמַר, וְחַרְבּוֹ שְׁלוּפָה בְּיָדוֹ נְטוּיָה עַל יְרוּשָׁלָיִם:

וּבְמֹרָא גָּדֹל, זוֹ גִּלּוּי שְׁכִינָה, כְּמָה שֶׁנֶּאֱמַר, אוֹ הֲנִסָּה אֱלֹהִים לָבוֹא לָקַחַת לוֹ גוֹי מִקֶּרֶב גּוֹי בְּמַסֹּת בְּאֹתֹת וּבְמוֹפְתִים וּבְמִלְחָמָה וּבְיָד חֲזָקָה וּבִזְרוֹעַ נְטוּיָה וּבְמוֹרָאִים גְּדֹלִים כְּכֹל אֲשֶׁר עָשָׂה לָכֶם יְהֹוָה אֱלֹהֵיכֶם בְּמִצְרַיִם לְעֵינֶיךָ:

With signs - this refers to the staff, as it says, "And take this staff in your hand, with which you will perform the signs" (*Shemos* 4:17).

וּבְאֹתוֹת, זֶה הַמַּטֶּה, כְּמָה שֶׁנֶּאֱמַר, וְאֶת הַמַּטֶּה הַזֶּה תִּקַּח בְּיָדֶךָ אֲשֶׁר תַּעֲשֶׂה בּוֹ אֶת הָאֹתֹת:

278. One should spill wine out of his cup when saying each of the words דם, ואש and עשן, when enumerating each of the ten plagues, and when saying the three acronyms, עד"ש, דצ"ך, באח"ב.

279. The index finger should be used. Nevertheless, some have the custom to use the little finger and some use the ring finger. If a person is too sensitive to use his finger, he should spill out the drops by tilting the cup.

280. When spilling the wine, one should have in mind that Hashem should protect us from such terrible plagues and bring them upon our enemies.

281. The spilled wine should be thrown away since an impure spirit rests on it.

282. If necessary, the cups should be refilled before saying 'Rabban Gamliel' etc.

With wonders - this refers to the blood, as it says, "I will show wonders in heaven and on earth: blood, fire, and columns of smoke" (*Yoel* 3:3).

וּבְמֹפְתִים, זֶה הַדָּם, כְּמָה שֶׁנֶּאֱמַר, וְנָתַתִּי מוֹפְתִים בַּשָּׁמַיִם וּבָאָרֶץ דָּם וָאֵשׁ וְתִימְרוֹת עָשָׁן:

An alternative explanation:

With a mighty hand - two (plagues).

An outstretched arm - two.

Great awe - two.

Signs - two.

Wonders - two.

דָּבָר אַחֵר,
בְּיָד חֲזָקָה שְׁתַּיִם,
וּבִזְרֹעַ נְטוּיָה שְׁתַּיִם,
וּבְמֹרָא גָּדֹל שְׁתַּיִם,
וּבְאֹתוֹת שְׁתַּיִם,
וּבְמֹפְתִים שְׁתַּיִם:

These are the ten plagues which the Holy one, blessed is He, brought upon the Egyptians in Egypt, as follows:

1. Blood. 2. Frogs. 3. Lice. 4. Wild beasts. 5. Pestilence. 6. Boils. 7. Hail. 8. Locusts. 9. Darkness. 10. Slaying of the firstborn.

אֵלּוּ עֶשֶׂר מַכּוֹת שֶׁהֵבִיא הַקָּדוֹשׁ בָּרוּךְ הוּא עַל הַמִּצְרִים בְּמִצְרַיִם, וְאֵלּוּ הֵן -

דָּם, צְפַרְדֵּעַ, כִּנִּים, עָרוֹב, דֶּבֶר, שְׁחִין, בָּרָד, אַרְבֶּה, חֹשֶׁךְ, מַכַּת בְּכוֹרוֹת:

Rabbi Yehuda abbreviated them by their Hebrew initials:

Detzach, Adash, Be'achav.

רַבִּי יְהוּדָה הָיָה נוֹתֵן בָּהֶם סִמָּנִים,

דְּצַ"ךְ, עֲדַ"שׁ, בְּאַחַ"ב:

Rabbi Yossi the Gallilean said, "Where is there proof that the Egyptians were struck with ten plagues in Egypt, but with fifty plagues at the sea? Concerning the plagues in Egypt, it says, 'And the sorcerers said to Pharaoh - 'it is the finger of God'" (*Shemos* 8:15). Concerning the events at the sea, it says, 'And Yisroel saw the great hand that Hashem used upon the Egyptians, and the people feared Hashem, and they believed in Hashem and in His servant Moshe' (*Shemos* 14:31). How many plagues did they receive with the finger? Ten! Thus, if they received ten plagues in Egypt, they must have received [with the hand] fifty at the sea!"

Rabbi Eliezer said, "Where is there proof that each plague that the Holy One, blessed is He, brought upon the Egyptians in Egypt, was fourfold? For it says, 'He sent upon them his fierce anger; wrath, and fury, and distress, a delegation of evil emissaries' (*Tehillim* 78:49).

רַבִּי יוֹסֵי הַגְּלִילִי אוֹמֵר, מִנַּיִן אַתָּה אוֹמֵר שֶׁלָּקוּ הַמִּצְרִים בְּמִצְרַיִם עֶשֶׂר מַכּוֹת וְעַל הַיָּם לָקוּ חֲמִשִּׁים מַכּוֹת. בְּמִצְרַיִם מָה הוּא אוֹמֵר, וַיֹּאמְרוּ הַחַרְטֻמִּם אֶל פַּרְעֹה אֶצְבַּע אֱלֹהִים הִוא. וְעַל הַיָּם מָה הוּא אוֹמֵר, וַיַּרְא יִשְׂרָאֵל אֶת הַיָּד הַגְּדֹלָה אֲשֶׁר עָשָׂה יְהֹוָה בְּמִצְרַיִם וַיִּירְאוּ הָעָם אֶת יְהֹוָה וַיַּאֲמִינוּ בַּיהֹוָה וּבְמֹשֶׁה עַבְדּוֹ: כַּמָּה לָקוּ בְאֶצְבַּע עֶשֶׂר מַכּוֹת. אֱמֹר מֵעַתָּה, בְּמִצְרַיִם לָקוּ עֶשֶׂר מַכּוֹת וְעַל הַיָּם לָקוּ חֲמִשִּׁים מַכּוֹת:

רַבִּי אֱלִיעֶזֶר אוֹמֵר, מִנַּיִן שֶׁכָּל מַכָּה וּמַכָּה שֶׁהֵבִיא הַקָּדוֹשׁ בָּרוּךְ הוּא עַל הַמִּצְרִים בְּמִצְרַיִם הָיְתָה שֶׁל אַרְבַּע מַכּוֹת, שֶׁנֶּאֱמַר, יְשַׁלַּח בָּם חֲרוֹן אַפּוֹ עֶבְרָה וָזַעַם וְצָרָה מִשְׁלַחַת מַלְאֲכֵי רָעִים:

Wrath - one; Fury - two; Distress - three; Delegation of evil emissaries - four. Thus conclude, that in Egypt they received forty plagues, and by the sea, two hundred plagues."

Rabbi Akiva said, "Where is there proof that each plague that the Holy one, blessed is He, brought upon the Egyptians in Egypt, was fivefold? For it says, 'He sent upon them his fierce anger, wrath, and fury, and distress, a delegation of evil emissaries' (Tehillim 78:49).

Fierce anger - one; Wrath - two; Fury - three; Distress - four; Delegation of evil emissaries - five. Thus conclude, that in Egypt they received fifty plagues, and by the sea, two hundred and fifty plagues."

עֶבְרָה, אַחַת. וָזַעַם, שְׁתַּיִם. וְצָרָה, שָׁלֹשׁ. מִשְׁלַחַת מַלְאֲכֵי רָעִים, אַרְבַּע. אֱמֹר מֵעַתָּה, בְּמִצְרַיִם לָקוּ אַרְבָּעִים מַכּוֹת וְעַל הַיָּם לָקוּ מָאתַיִם מַכּוֹת:

רַבִּי עֲקִיבָא אוֹמֵר, מִנַּיִן שֶׁכָּל מַכָּה וּמַכָּה שֶׁהֵבִיא הַקָּדוֹשׁ בָּרוּךְ הוּא עַל הַמִּצְרִים בְּמִצְרַיִם הָיְתָה שֶׁל חָמֵשׁ מַכּוֹת, שֶׁנֶּאֱמַר, יְשַׁלַּח בָּם חֲרוֹן אַפּוֹ עֶבְרָה וָזַעַם וְצָרָה מִשְׁלַחַת מַלְאֲכֵי רָעִים:

חֲרוֹן אַפּוֹ, אַחַת. עֶבְרָה, שְׁתַּיִם. וָזַעַם, שָׁלֹשׁ. וְצָרָה, אַרְבַּע. מִשְׁלַחַת מַלְאֲכֵי רָעִים, חָמֵשׁ. אֱמֹר מֵעַתָּה, בְּמִצְרַיִם לָקוּ חֲמִשִּׁים מַכּוֹת וְעַל הַיָּם לָקוּ חֲמִשִּׁים וּמָאתַיִם מַכּוֹת:

How many great praises do we owe to the Omnipresent!

If He had taken us out of Egypt and not executed judgments against the Egyptians, this would have been a sufficient reason to thank Him.

If He had executed judgments against the Egyptians and not against their gods, this would have been a sufficient reason to thank Him.

If He had executed judgment against their gods and not slain their firstborn, this would have been a sufficient reason to thank Him.

If He had slain their firstborn and not given us their wealth, this would have been a sufficient reason to thank Him.

If he had given us their wealth and not split the sea for us, this would have been a sufficient reason to thank Him.

If he had split the sea for us and not led us through it on dry land, this would have been a sufficient reason to thank Him.

כַּמָּה מַעֲלוֹת טוֹבוֹת לַמָּקוֹם עָלֵינוּ:

אִלּוּ הוֹצִיאָנוּ מִמִּצְרַיִם וְלֹא עָשָׂה בָהֶם שְׁפָטִים, דַּיֵּנוּ.

אִלּוּ עָשָׂה בָהֶם שְׁפָטִים וְלֹא עָשָׂה בֵאלֹהֵיהֶם, דַּיֵּנוּ.

אִלּוּ עָשָׂה בֵאלֹהֵיהֶם וְלֹא הָרַג אֶת בְּכוֹרֵיהֶם, דַּיֵּנוּ.

אִלּוּ הָרַג אֶת בְּכוֹרֵיהֶם וְלֹא נָתַן לָנוּ אֶת מָמוֹנָם, דַּיֵּנוּ.

אִלּוּ נָתַן לָנוּ אֶת מָמוֹנָם וְלֹא קָרַע לָנוּ אֶת הַיָּם, דַּיֵּנוּ.

אִלּוּ קָרַע לָנוּ אֶת הַיָּם וְלֹא הֶעֱבִירָנוּ בְתוֹכוֹ בֶּחָרָבָה, דַּיֵּנוּ.

If He had led us through the sea on dry land and not drowned our oppressors in it, this would have been a sufficient reason to thank Him.

If He had drowned our oppressors in the sea and not provided our needs in the desert for forty years, this would have been a sufficient reason to thank Him.

If He had provided our needs in the desert for forty years and not fed us with manna, this would have been a sufficient reason to thank Him.

If he had fed us with manna and not given us the Shabbos, this would have been a sufficient reason to thank Him.

If he had given us the Shabbos and not brought us to Har Sinai, this would have been a sufficient reason to thank Him.

If He had brought us to Har Sinai and not given us the Torah, this would have been a sufficient reason to thank Him.

If he had given us the Torah and not brought us into *Eretz Yisroel*, this would have been a sufficient reason to thank Him.

If He had brought us into *Eretz Yisroel* and not built the *Beis Hamikdash* for us, this would have been a sufficient reason to thank Him.

אִלּוּ הֶעֱבִירָנוּ בְּתוֹכוֹ בֶּחָרָבָה וְלֹא שִׁקַּע צָרֵינוּ בְּתוֹכוֹ, דַּיֵּנוּ.

אִלּוּ שִׁקַּע צָרֵינוּ בְּתוֹכוֹ וְלֹא סִפֵּק צָרְכֵּינוּ בַּמִּדְבָּר אַרְבָּעִים שָׁנָה, דַּיֵּנוּ.

אִלּוּ סִפֵּק צָרְכֵּינוּ בַּמִּדְבָּר אַרְבָּעִים שָׁנָה וְלֹא הֶאֱכִילָנוּ אֶת הַמָּן, דַּיֵּנוּ.

אִלּוּ הֶאֱכִילָנוּ אֶת הַמָּן וְלֹא נָתַן לָנוּ אֶת הַשַּׁבָּת, דַּיֵּנוּ.

אִלּוּ נָתַן לָנוּ אֶת הַשַּׁבָּת וְלֹא קֵרְבָנוּ לִפְנֵי הַר סִינַי, דַּיֵּנוּ.

אִלּוּ קֵרְבָנוּ לִפְנֵי הַר סִינַי וְלֹא נָתַן לָנוּ אֶת הַתּוֹרָה, דַּיֵּנוּ.

אִלּוּ נָתַן לָנוּ אֶת הַתּוֹרָה וְלֹא הִכְנִיסָנוּ לְאֶרֶץ יִשְׂרָאֵל, דַּיֵּנוּ.

אִלּוּ הִכְנִיסָנוּ לְאֶרֶץ יִשְׂרָאֵל וְלֹא בָנָה לָנוּ אֶת בֵּית הַבְּחִירָה, דַּיֵּנוּ.

Therefore, how much more so are we indebted to thank the Omnipresent for all the manifold favors: He took us out of Egypt, and executed judgments against the Egyptians, and against their gods, and slew their firstborn, and gave us their wealth, and split the sea for us, and led us through it on dry land, and drowned our oppressors in it, and provided our needs in the desert for forty years, and fed us with manna, and gave us the Shabbos, and brought us to Har Sinai, and gave us the Torah, and brought us into *Eretz Yisroel*, and built for us the *Beis Hamikdash* to atone for all our sins.

עַל אַחַת כַּמָּה וְכַמָּה טוֹבָה כְפוּלָה וּמְכֻפֶּלֶת לַמָּקוֹם עָלֵינוּ, שֶׁהוֹצִיאָנוּ מִמִּצְרַיִם, וְעָשָׂה בָהֶם שְׁפָטִים, וְעָשָׂה בֵאלֹהֵיהֶם, וְהָרַג אֶת בְּכוֹרֵיהֶם, וְנָתַן לָנוּ אֶת מָמוֹנָם, וְקָרַע לָנוּ אֶת הַיָּם, וְהֶעֱבִירָנוּ בְתוֹכוֹ בֶּחָרָבָה, וְשִׁקַּע צָרֵינוּ בְּתוֹכוֹ, וְסִפֵּק צָרְכֵּנוּ בַּמִּדְבָּר אַרְבָּעִים שָׁנָה, וְהֶאֱכִילָנוּ אֶת הַמָּן, וְנָתַן לָנוּ אֶת הַשַּׁבָּת, וְקֵרְבָנוּ לִפְנֵי הַר סִינַי, וְנָתַן לָנוּ אֶת הַתּוֹרָה, וְהִכְנִיסָנוּ לְאֶרֶץ יִשְׂרָאֵל, וּבָנָה לָנוּ אֶת בֵּית הַבְּחִירָה לְכַפֵּר עַל כָּל עֲוֹנוֹתֵינוּ:

Rabban Gamliel used to say, "Whoever has not explained the following three things on Pesach night, has not fulfilled his obligation. Namely:

Pesach, Matza, and *Maror*."

רַבָּן גַּמְלִיאֵל הָיָה אוֹמֵר,
כָּל שֶׁלֹּא אָמַר שְׁלֹשָׁה דְבָרִים אֵלּוּ בַּפֶּסַח
לֹא יָצָא יְדֵי חוֹבָתוֹ, וְאֵלּוּ הֵן:
פֶּסַח, מַצָּה, וּמָרוֹר:

When saying פסח שהיו *etc., the piece of roast meat should not be held since this would appear as if he is dedicating it as the Korban Pesach. However, the custom is to look at it.*

The *Korban Pesach* that our fathers used to eat when the *Beis Hamikdash* stood - for what reason?

Because the Holy One, blessed is He, passed over the houses of our forefathers in Egypt, as it says, "And you shall say, 'It is a Pesach offering to Hashem, Who passed over the houses of the children of Yisroel in Egypt when He struck the Egyptians and spared our houses, and the people bowed and prostrated themselves'" (Shemos 12:27).

פֶּסַח שֶׁהָיוּ אֲבוֹתֵינוּ אוֹכְלִים בִּזְמַן
שֶׁבֵּית הַמִּקְדָּשׁ הָיָה קַיָּם, עַל שׁוּם מָה.
עַל שׁוּם שֶׁפָּסַח הַקָּדוֹשׁ בָּרוּךְ הוּא עַל
בָּתֵּי אֲבוֹתֵינוּ בְּמִצְרַיִם. שֶׁנֶּאֱמַר, וַאֲמַרְתֶּם
זֶבַח פֶּסַח הוּא לַיהֹוָה אֲשֶׁר פָּסַח עַל בָּתֵּי
בְנֵי יִשְׂרָאֵל בְּמִצְרַיִם בְּנָגְפּוֹ אֶת מִצְרַיִם
וְאֶת בָּתֵּינוּ הִצִּיל וַיִּקֹּד הָעָם וַיִּשְׁתַּחֲווּ:

When saying מַצָּה זוּ etc., the leader of the Seder should hold up the broken middle matza.

This Matza that we eat - for what reason?

Because the dough of our forefathers did not have time to rise, before the King of kings, the Holy One, blessed is He, revealed Himself to them and redeemed them, as it says, "And they baked the dough that they had brought out of Egypt into cakes of matza, for it had not fermented, because they were driven out of Egypt and could not delay, and could not even prepare provisions for the way" (Shemos 12:39).

מַצָּה זוּ שֶׁאָנוּ אוֹכְלִים עַל שׁוּם מָה. עַל שׁוּם שֶׁלֹּא הִסְפִּיק בְּצֵקָם שֶׁל אֲבוֹתֵינוּ לְהַחֲמִיץ, עַד שֶׁנִּגְלָה עֲלֵיהֶם מֶלֶךְ מַלְכֵי הַמְּלָכִים הַקָּדוֹשׁ בָּרוּךְ הוּא וּגְאָלָם, שֶׁנֶּאֱמַר, וַיֹּאפוּ אֶת הַבָּצֵק אֲשֶׁר הוֹצִיאוּ מִמִּצְרַיִם עֻגֹת מַצּוֹת כִּי לֹא חָמֵץ, כִּי גֹרְשׁוּ מִמִּצְרַיִם וְלֹא יָכְלוּ לְהִתְמַהְמֵהַּ וְגַם צֵדָה לֹא עָשׂוּ לָהֶם:

	The Guidelines Haggadah

When saying מרור זה etc, the leader of the Seder should hold up the Maror.

This *Maror* that we eat - for what reason?

Because the Egyptians embittered the lives of our forefathers in Egypt, as it says, "And they embittered their lives with hard labor, with mortar and bricks, and with all manner of work in the field; all their work that they forced them to do with crushing labor" (*Shemos* 1:14).

מָרוֹר זֶה שֶׁאָנוּ אוֹכְלִים עַל שׁוּם מָה. עַל שׁוּם שֶׁמֵּרְרוּ הַמִּצְרִים אֶת חַיֵּי אֲבוֹתֵינוּ בְּמִצְרַיִם, שֶׁנֶּאֱמַר, וַיְמָרְרוּ אֶת חַיֵּיהֶם בַּעֲבֹדָה קָשָׁה בְּחֹמֶר וּבִלְבֵנִים וּבְכָל עֲבֹדָה בַּשָּׂדֶה, אֵת כָּל עֲבֹדָתָם אֲשֶׁר עָבְדוּ בָהֶם בְּפָרֶךְ:

When saying the paragraph בכל דור ודור, one should try to visualize himself in Egypt enduring harsh slavery and then being redeemed miraculously by Hashem.

In every generation, one is obligated to see oneself as if he personally went out of Egypt, as it says, "And you shall tell your son on that day, saying, 'It is because of this (service) that Hashem acted for me when I went out of Egypt'" (*Shemos* 13:8). The Holy One, blessed is He, not only redeemed our forefathers from

בְּכָל דּוֹר וָדוֹר חַיָּב אָדָם לִרְאוֹת אֶת עַצְמוֹ כְּאִלּוּ הוּא יָצָא מִמִּצְרַיִם. שֶׁנֶּאֱמַר, וְהִגַּדְתָּ לְבִנְךָ בַּיּוֹם הַהוּא לֵאמֹר בַּעֲבוּר זֶה עָשָׂה יְהֹוָה לִי בְּצֵאתִי מִמִּצְרָיִם. לֹא אֶת אֲבוֹתֵינוּ בִּלְבָד גָּאַל הַקָּדוֹשׁ בָּרוּךְ הוּא, אֶלָּא אַף אוֹתָנוּ גָּאַל עִמָּהֶם.

slavery, but He also redeemed us with them, as it says, "And He took us out from there, to bring us to the land that He swore to our forefathers to give us"

(*Devarim* 6:23).

שֶׁנֶּאֱמַר, וְאוֹתָנוּ הוֹצִיא מִשָּׁם, לְמַעַן הָבִיא אוֹתָנוּ לָתֶת לָנוּ אֶת הָאָרֶץ אֲשֶׁר נִשְׁבַּע לַאֲבוֹתֵינוּ:

> *If possible, the wine should be held from the start of the paragraph לפיכך until the wine is drunk. The matzos should be covered during this time. If it will be difficult to hold the wine for this length of time, one should hold the wine from the start of Hallel. If this is also difficult, it is sufficient to hold the wine from the start of the b'racha אשר גאלנו.*

Therefore, it is our duty to thank, laud, praise, glorify, exalt, honor, bless, extol, and acclaim the One Who performed all these miracles for our forefathers and for us. He brought us from slavery to freedom, from grief to joy, from mourning to festivity, from darkness to great light, and from servitude to redemption. Let us therefore recite a new song before Him, Halleluyah!

לְפִיכָךְ אֲנַחְנוּ חַיָּבִים לְהוֹדוֹת לְהַלֵּל לְשַׁבֵּחַ לְפָאֵר לְרוֹמֵם לְהַדֵּר לְבָרֵךְ לְעַלֵּה וּלְקַלֵּס לְמִי שֶׁעָשָׂה לַאֲבוֹתֵינוּ וְלָנוּ אֶת כָּל הַנִּסִּים הָאֵלֶּה. הוֹצִיאָנוּ מֵעַבְדוּת לְחֵרוּת, מִיָּגוֹן לְשִׂמְחָה, מֵאֵבֶל לְיוֹם טוֹב, וּמֵאֲפֵלָה לְאוֹר גָּדוֹל, וּמִשִּׁעְבּוּד לִגְאֻלָּה, וְנֹאמַר לְפָנָיו שִׁירָה חֲדָשָׁה הַלְלוּיָהּ:

> *Before reciting Hallel, one should think that he is about to fulfill the*
> *Rabbinic mitzvah of reciting Hallel.*

Halleluyah! Servants of Hashem, praise Him; praise the name of Hashem. May the name of Hashem be blessed from now and forever. From the rising of the sun until it sets, praised is Hashem's name. Hashem is high above all nations, above the heavens is His glory. Who is like Hashem our God Who dwells on high, Who lowers Himself to look upon the heavens and the earth? He raises the needy from the dust; from the trash heaps He lifts up the destitute, to seat them with nobles, with the nobles of His people. He transforms the barren woman to a joyful mother, Halleluyah!

הַלְלוּיָהּ, הַלְלוּ עַבְדֵי יְהוָה, הַלְלוּ אֶת שֵׁם יְהוָה: יְהִי שֵׁם יְהוָה מְבֹרָךְ, מֵעַתָּה וְעַד עוֹלָם: מִמִּזְרַח שֶׁמֶשׁ עַד מְבוֹאוֹ, מְהֻלָּל שֵׁם יְהוָה: רָם עַל כָּל גּוֹיִם יְהוָה, עַל הַשָּׁמַיִם כְּבוֹדוֹ: מִי כַּיהוָה אֱלֹהֵינוּ, הַמַּגְבִּיהִי לָשָׁבֶת: הַמַּשְׁפִּילִי לִרְאוֹת, בַּשָּׁמַיִם וּבָאָרֶץ: מְקִימִי מֵעָפָר דָּל, מֵאַשְׁפֹּת יָרִים אֶבְיוֹן: לְהוֹשִׁיבִי עִם נְדִיבִים, עִם נְדִיבֵי עַמּוֹ: מוֹשִׁיבִי עֲקֶרֶת הַבַּיִת, אֵם הַבָּנִים שְׂמֵחָה, הַלְלוּיָהּ:

The Guidelines Haggadah

When Yisroel went out of Egypt, the house of Yaakov from a foreign people. Yehudah became His sanctifier, Yisroel His dominions. The sea saw and fled, the Jordan turned back. The mountains skipped like rams, the hills like lambs. What troubles you, O sea that you flee, O Jordan that you turn back, O mountains that you skip like rams, O hills like lambs? Before Hashem who created the earth, before the God of Yaakov, Who turns the rock into a pool of water, the flintstone into a spring of water.

בְּצֵאת יִשְׂרָאֵל מִמִּצְרָיִם, בֵּית יַעֲקֹב מֵעַם לֹעֵז: הָיְתָה יְהוּדָה לְקָדְשׁוֹ יִשְׂרָאֵל מַמְשְׁלוֹתָיו: הַיָּם רָאָה וַיָּנֹס, הַיַּרְדֵּן יִסֹּב לְאָחוֹר: הֶהָרִים רָקְדוּ כְאֵילִים, גְּבָעוֹת כִּבְנֵי צֹאן: מַה לְּךָ הַיָּם כִּי תָנוּס, הַיַּרְדֵּן תִּסֹּב לְאָחוֹר: הֶהָרִים תִּרְקְדוּ כְאֵילִים, גְּבָעוֹת כִּבְנֵי צֹאן: מִלִּפְנֵי אָדוֹן חוּלִי אָרֶץ מִלִּפְנֵי אֱלוֹהַּ יַעֲקֹב: הַהֹפְכִי הַצּוּר אֲגַם מָיִם, חַלָּמִישׁ לְמַעְיְנוֹ מָיִם:

Before drinking the second cup of wine, one should think that he is about to fulfill the mitzvah of drinking the second of the four cups of wine.

If he intends to drink wine or grape juice during the meal, he should have in mind to include it with the b'racha recited on this second cup.

Men should remember that they must recline when drinking the wine.

If a man forgot to recline, he should immediately drink another cup without a b'racha.

Blessed are You, Hashem our God, King of the universe, Who redeemed us and redeemed our forefathers from Egypt, and enabled us to reach this night to eat matza and *Maror*. So too, Hashem our God, and God of our forefathers, bring us to other future holidays and festivals in peace, rejoicing in the rebuilding of Your city and happy in Your service. And there we shall eat of the offerings and of the *Korban Pesach*, whose blood will pleasingly reach the side of Your Altar. And we shall thank You with a new song for our redemption and for the deliverance of our souls. Blessed are You Hashem, Who redeemed Yisroel.

Blessed are You, Hashem our God, King of the universe, Who creates the fruit of the vine.

בָּרוּךְ אַתָּה יְיָ אֱלֹהֵינוּ מֶלֶךְ הָעוֹלָם, אֲשֶׁר גְּאָלָנוּ וְגָאַל אֶת אֲבוֹתֵינוּ מִמִּצְרַיִם, וְהִגִּיעָנוּ הַלַּיְלָה הַזֶּה לֶאֱכָל בּוֹ מַצָּה וּמָרוֹר. כֵּן יְיָ אֱלֹהֵינוּ וֵאלֹהֵי אֲבוֹתֵינוּ יַגִּיעֵנוּ לְמוֹעֲדִים וְלִרְגָלִים אֲחֵרִים הַבָּאִים לִקְרָאתֵנוּ לְשָׁלוֹם, שְׂמֵחִים בְּבִנְיַן עִירֶךָ, וְשָׂשִׂים בַּעֲבוֹדָתֶךָ, וְנֹאכַל שָׁם מִן הַזְּבָחִים וּמִן הַפְּסָחִים אֲשֶׁר יַגִּיעַ דָּמָם עַל קִיר מִזְבַּחֲךָ לְרָצוֹן וְנוֹדֶה לְךָ שִׁיר חָדָשׁ עַל גְּאֻלָּתֵנוּ וְעַל פְּדוּת נַפְשֵׁנוּ: בָּרוּךְ אַתָּה יְיָ גָּאַל יִשְׂרָאֵל:

בָּרוּךְ אַתָּה יְיָ אֱלֹהֵינוּ מֶלֶךְ הָעוֹלָם, בּוֹרֵא פְּרִי הַגָּפֶן:

The Guidelines Haggadah

רָחְצָה

Rochtza

Wash the hands

283. Although the hands were washed at the beginning of the Seder (*Urchatz*), they are now washed again before eating the matza.

284. The *b'racha Al Netilas Yadayim* is recited.

285. If a person is sure that his hands have not become *tamei* since the first washing, he should deliberately make his hands *tamei* before washing now. This can be done by scratching one's scalp.

286. Before washing the hands, the leader of the Seder should announce that one may not speak after washing the hands, unless it concerns the mitzvos, until after *Korech*.

287. He should inform everyone about the next few steps of the Seder, and tell them the relevant laws.

288. Each person should be given a piece of matza weighing at least 25 grams in preparation for the mitzvah of eating matza.

289. Children may be given 10 grams each.

290. The steps *Rochtza*, *Motzi*, and *Matza* should be announced.

291. Some have the custom to ask one of the children to wash the hands of the father, in order to demonstrate freedom and royalty.

Blessed are You, Hashem our God, King of the universe, Who has sanctified us with His commandments and commanded us to wash the hands.

בָּרוּךְ אַתָּה יְיָ אֱלֹהֵינוּ מֶלֶךְ הָעוֹלָם, אֲשֶׁר קִדְּשָׁנוּ בְּמִצְוֹתָיו, וְצִוָּנוּ עַל נְטִילַת יָדָיִם:

מוֹצִיא מַצָּה

Motzi - Matza

Two brachos are recited for the Matza

292. Before the *brachos* are recited, the leader of the Seder should have in mind to include everyone else with his *brachos*.

293. Everyone else should have in mind to fulfill his obligation by listening to the *brachos*.

294. Everyone should have in mind to fulfill the Torah mitzvah to eat matza on the first night of Pesach (Rabbinic on the second night).

295. Everyone should have in mind that the *brachos* should also apply to the *Korech* and *Afikoman*.

296. The men should remember to recline while eating the matza.

297. The matzos should be covered with a cloth while the *b'racha* of *Hamotzi* is recited and then uncovered.

298. The first *b'racha* is the regular *b'racha* of *Hamotzi* recited over bread or matza.

299. The second *b'racha* - *Al Achilas Matza* - is recited for the mitzvah of eating matza on the night of Pesach.

300. All three matzos should be held for the first *b'racha*, after which the lowest matza is released. The remaining two matzos are held for the second *b'racha*.

301. Ideally, the two matzos should be broken simultaneously.

302. The leader of the Seder should take for himself 15 grams from the top matza and 15 grams from the middle one. Both pieces should be eaten together.

303. Everyone else should be given a small piece from the top matza in addition to the

prepared piece of 25 grams that was distributed before washing. Both pieces should be eaten together.

304. The main custom is not to dip the matza in salt.

305. The matza should be eaten as quickly as possible, ideally within two minutes. If this is difficult, it may be eaten within four minutes. This is measured from the time that one begins to swallow the matza. One should nevertheless not eat in a state of frenzy or with voracity, but rather with dignity and joy as one fulfills the commandment of Hashem. A person who did not succeed in eating the matza within four

minutes, should preferably eat another *kezayis* within this time.

306. If one's mouth is too dry to swallow the matza, one may drink a little water with it to facilitate swallowing.

307. If a man forgot to recline while eating the matza, he must eat another *kezayis* while reclining. No *b'racha* is recited, but care should be taken not to speak before eating this matza.

308. If one ate the matza without intention to fulfill the mitzvah, one should eat another *kezayis* with the correct intention. No *b'racha* is recited.

Blessed are You, Hashem our God, King of the universe, Who brings out bread from the earth.

Blessed are You, Hashem our God, King of the universe, Who has sanctified us with His commandments and commanded us to eat matza.

בָּרוּךְ אַתָּה יְיָ אֱלֹהֵינוּ מֶלֶךְ הָעוֹלָם, הַמּוֹצִיא לֶחֶם מִן הָאָרֶץ:

בָּרוּךְ אַתָּה יְיָ אֱלֹהֵינוּ מֶלֶךְ הָעוֹלָם, אֲשֶׁר קִדְּשָׁנוּ בְּמִצְוֹתָיו, וְצִוָּנוּ עַל אֲכִילַת מַצָּה:

מָרוֹר

Maror

Eat the bitter herbs

309. If lettuce is used for *Maror*, one should take a leaf that measures 12" long and 5½" at the widest point.

310. If grated horseradish is used, one should eat 27cc if possible. If this is difficult, it is sufficient to eat 17cc (approx. one heaped tablespoon).

311. Since both lettuce and horseradish are suitable species, one may combine them to make the required amount. Some have the custom to do this in order to feel some bitter taste since the lettuce is not usually bitter.

312. The *Maror* should be eaten as quickly as possible but in no more than four minutes. This is measured from the time that one begins to swallow.

313. Since certain species of *Maror* contain a bitter juice, the *Maror* is dipped into sweet *charoses* in order to neutralize this. In addition, the *charoses* is a reminder of the mortar used by the Jewish slaves.

314. It is sufficient to dip some of the *Maror* in *charoses*.

315. Although the *charoses* is initially made thick to resemble mortar, it should be diluted considerably at this stage, making it suitable for dipping by adding more wine. The wine is also a reminder of the Jewish blood that was spilled copiously during the years of hard labor.

316. The custom is for each person to recite his own *b'racha* for the *Maror*.

317. Before reciting the *b'racha Al Achilas*

Maror, one should think that the *b'racha* should also apply to the *Korech*, and that one is about to fulfill the Rabbinic mitzvah of eating *Maror*.

318. If one ate the *Maror* without the intention to fulfill the mitzvah, he should preferably eat another *kezayis*.

319. One does not recline while eating *Maror* since it is a reminder of slavery and not of freedom.

320. If one wishes to remove the sharpness of the horseradish from one's mouth, he should drink some hot water. This is a proven remedy.

Blessed are You, Hashem our God, King of the universe, Who has sanctified us with His commandments and commanded us to eat *Maror*.

בָּרוּךְ אַתָּה יְיָ אֱלֹהֵינוּ מֶלֶךְ הָעוֹלָם, אֲשֶׁר קִדְּשָׁנוּ בְּמִצְוֹתָיו, וְצִוָּנוּ עַל אֲכִילַת מָרוֹר:

Korech

Eat the Sandwich of Matza and Maror

321. Although the vast majority of the Rabbis said that matza and *Maror* should be eaten separately, it was the opinion of Hillel that they should be eaten together. On the Seder night, we wish to fulfill both opinions and therefore we eat them first separately and then together.

322. The bottom matza should be used. If this is not sufficient for everyone, the leader of the Seder should distribute to each person a small piece from this matza and supplement it with other matza to make the required quantity.

323. Each person should have 15 grams of matza for *Korech*.

324. The amount of *Maror* used for *Korech* should be the same amount that was used for *Maror*.

325. There are different customs regarding the dipping of *Maror* in *charoses*, but the main custom is to dip it.

326. The custom is to place the *Maror* between two pieces of matza.

327. A *b'racha* is not recited for *Korech*, but a paragraph is said beginning with the words זכר למקדש כהלל. Although some opinions prefer the recital of this paragraph after eating the sandwich, the widespread custom is to recite it before eating the sandwich.

328. If possible, the sandwich should be eaten within four minutes and if necessary within nine minutes. This is measured from the time one begins to swallow.

The Guidelines Haggadah

329. A man should recline when eating the sandwich.

330. If a man forgot to recline, he does not need to eat another sandwich.

In remembrance of the *Beis Hamikdash*, according to the opinion of Hillel.

When the *Beis Hamikdash* stood, Hillel would combine matza and *Maror* and eat them together, to fufill the verse, "They should eat it with matza and *Maror*" (*Bamidbar* 9:11).

זֵכֶר לְמִקְדָּשׁ כְּהִלֵּל.

כֵּן עָשָׂה הִלֵּל, בִּזְמַן שֶׁבֵּית הַמִּקְדָּשׁ הָיָה קַיָּם, הָיָה כּוֹרֵךְ מַצָּה וּמָרוֹר וְאוֹכֵל בְּיַחַד, לְקַיֵּם מַה שֶׁנֶּאֱמַר, עַל מַצּוֹת וּמְרֹרִים יֹאכְלֻהוּ:

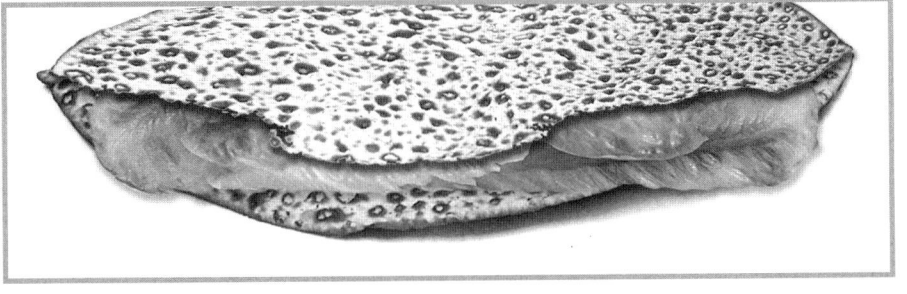

שֻׁלְחָן עוֹרֵךְ

Shulchan - Orech

Eat the Yom Tov meal

331. Most have the custom to begin the meal by first serving the egg from the Seder plate. Some dip it in salt water. Some do not eat this egg. Some have the custom to serve other eggs.

332. Some have a custom to eat fish as a reminder that Hashem miraculously provided the Jewish women with fish when they drew water for their exhausted husbands in *Mitzrayim*.

333. Roast meat or poultry must not be served. The meat from the Seder plate must also not be eaten.

334. One should not eat excessively. Overeating may cause drowsiness and he will not be able to conclude the Seder successfully. One must also remain with some appetite for the *Afikoman* at the end of the meal.

335. One must leave sufficient time after the meal to eat the *Afikoman* before *halachic* midnight.

336. If a dessert is served, one should avoid a fruit whose *b'racha* is *Borei Pri Ha'adama* since this raises a doubt whether the *b'racha* recited for the *Karpas* includes such a dessert.

337. It is praiseworthy for a man to recline during the meal but not a requirement. Most men do not do so since today we are not accustomed to recline, and it is difficult for us to eat comfortably and joyously in such a position.

338. According to some opinions, it is a mitzvah to drink some wine during the meal in honor of Yom Tov.

339. If the *charoses* is eaten together with matza or other food during the meal, a *b'racha* is not required. If it is eaten on its own, a *b'racha* is required. If the fruit is recognizable the *b'racha* is *Borei Pri Ha'eitz*, but if the fruit is not recognizable, the *b'racha* is *Shehakol*.

The Guidelines Haggadah

צָפוּן

Tzafun

Eat the Afikoman

340. *Afikoman* means dessert. The last item of food eaten at the Seder meal is a piece of matza called the *Afikoman*.

341. The word *'tzafun'* means hidden since the matza is put away at the beginning of the Seder and reserved for *Afikoman*.

342. In the days of the *Beis Hamikdash*, the last item of food eaten at the Seder meal was the *Korban Pesach*. Today, the *Afikoman* matza is eaten instead as a reminder of the *Korban Pesach*.

343. The piece of the broken middle matza that was put aside at the beginning of the Seder is eaten for the *Afikoman*. Since this is usually not sufficient for everyone, the leader of the Seder should distribute to each person a small piece

from this matza and supplement it with other matza to make the required quantity.

344. If the children have hidden the *Afikoman*, the custom is for the father to offer a reward for its return. This is to demonstrate how precious is a mitzvah.

345. If the *Afikoman* matza cannot be found, any other *shemura* matza should be used.

346. If possible, each person should eat two *kezaysim* (30 grams). If this is difficult, he may eat one *kezayis* (15 or 10 grams).

347. In the days of the *Beis Hamikdash*, the *Korban Pesach* was eaten together with matza. Therefore, we eat one *kezayis* of matza to remind us of the *Korban Pesach* and another

kezayis to remind us of the matza that was eaten together with the *Korban Pesach*.

348. A *b'racha* is not recited for the *Afikoman*, but one should have in mind to fulfill the mitzvah of eating the *Afikoman*. Before eating the *Afikoman*, some have a custom to recite a description of how the *Korban Pesach* was prepared and eaten.

349. A man should recline when eating the *Afikoman*.

350. If a man forgot to recline and has not yet washed his hands for *mayim acharonim*, he should eat another *Afikoman* if this is not too difficult. If he has already washed hands for *mayim acharonim*, he should not eat another *Afikoman*.

351. Effort should be made to eat the *Afikoman* before *halachic* midnight. Nevertheless, if this time passed, the *Afikoman* should still be eaten.

352. If one forgot to eat the *Afikoman*, it should be eaten immediately if he has not yet *bensched*. This is even if he has already washed

mayim acharonim. If he has *bensched* but not yet drunk the third cup of wine, he should wash hands without a *b'racha*, recite *Hamotzi*, eat the *Afikoman* and *bensch* again. If he has already drunk the third cup of wine, he should proceed as in the previous case, except that he should *bensch* without a cup of wine. This should be done even if he has already drunk the fourth cup of wine.

353. One may not eat anything else after the *Afikoman* so that the taste remains in the mouth for the rest of the night.

354. If a person ate something after the *Afikoman*, he must eat another *Afikoman* if possible.

355. Aside from the last two cups of wine one may not drink anything except for water after the *Afikoman*. Indeed, it is recommended to drink water after the *Afikoman* if one is thirsty since a person should not *bensch* while he is thirsty. One should preferably refrain from any other drinks, but in a case of great need one may drink tea, seltzer or lightly flavored soda. Coffee should not be drunk.

Barech

B e n s c h

356. The third cup of wine is poured before *bensching*. The cups should first be rinsed out.

357. Even if a person is lenient about washing *mayim acharonim* during the year, he should be particular to wash at the Seder since it is a night of extreme holiness.

358. If there are three men present, the custom is for the head of the household to lead the *zimun*. If there is an important visitor, he may be given this honor.

359. Before *bensching*, a man should think that he is about to fulfill the Torah mitzvah of *bensching*.

360. According to some opinions, everyone should hold the wine during *bensching*. According to other opinions, this is necessary only when there is no *zimun*, but when there is *zimun* only the leader needs to hold his wine.

361. Ideally, the wine should be held throughout the entire *bensching* until it is drunk. If this is difficult, it may be put down after *al yechasreinu*, and picked up again before reciting the *b'racha* over the wine.

A song of ascents. When Hashem will return the captives of Zion, we will have been like dreamers. Then our mouth will be filled with laughter and our tongue with joyous song. Then they will say among the nations, "Hashem has done great things with these". Hashem has done great things with us, we remained happy. Hashem! Return our captives like springs in the desert. Those who sow in tears will reap in joyous song. Though he who bears the measure of seed walks along weeping, he will return in joyous song bearing his sheaves.

שִׁיר הַמַּעֲלוֹת, בְּשׁוּב יְהֹוָה אֶת שִׁיבַת צִיּוֹן הָיִינוּ כְּחֹלְמִים: אָז יִמָּלֵא שְׂחוֹק פִּינוּ וּלְשׁוֹנֵנוּ רִנָּה, אָז יֹאמְרוּ בַגּוֹיִם הִגְדִּיל יְהֹוָה לַעֲשׂוֹת עִם אֵלֶּה: הִגְדִּיל יְהֹוָה לַעֲשׂוֹת עִמָּנוּ הָיִינוּ שְׂמֵחִים: שׁוּבָה יְהֹוָה אֶת שְׁבִיתֵנוּ כַּאֲפִיקִים בַּנֶּגֶב: הַזֹּרְעִים בְּדִמְעָה בְּרִנָּה יִקְצֹרוּ: הָלוֹךְ יֵלֵךְ וּבָכֹה נֹשֵׂא מֶשֶׁךְ הַזָּרַע בֹּא יָבֹא בְרִנָּה נֹשֵׂא אֲלֻמֹּתָיו:

> **If three men are present, recite the following.**
> **If ten men are present, add the words in brackets.**

Leader:	Gentlemen, let us *bensch*!
Others:	Blessed be the Name of Hashem from now and forever.
Leader:	Blessed be the Name of Hashem from now and forever. With your permission, my masters, Rabbis and teachers, let us bless (our God) the One Whose food we have eaten.
Others:	Blessed is (our God) the One Whose food we have eaten and through Whose goodness we live.
Leader:	Blessed is (our God) the One Whose food we have eaten and through Whose goodness we live. Blessed is He and blessed is His name.

Leader: רַבּוֹתַי נְבָרֵךְ:

Others: יְהִי שֵׁם יְהֹוָה מְבֹרָךְ מֵעַתָּה וְעַד עוֹלָם:

Leader: יְהִי שֵׁם יְהֹוָה מְבֹרָךְ מֵעַתָּה וְעַד עוֹלָם:
בִּרְשׁוּת מָרָנָן וְרַבָּנָן וְרַבּוֹתַי, נְבָרֵךְ (אֱלֹהֵינוּ) שֶׁאָכַלְנוּ מִשֶּׁלּוֹ:

Others: בָּרוּךְ (אֱלֹהֵינוּ) שֶׁאָכַלְנוּ מִשֶּׁלּוֹ וּבְטוּבוֹ חָיִינוּ:

Leader: בָּרוּךְ (אֱלֹהֵינוּ) שֶׁאָכַלְנוּ מִשֶּׁלּוֹ וּבְטוּבוֹ חָיִינוּ:
בָּרוּךְ הוּא וּבָרוּךְ שְׁמוֹ:

Blessed are You, Hashem our God, King of the universe, Who nourishes the entire world with His goodness, with favor, with kindness and with mercy. He gives food to all flesh, for His kindness endures forever. And through His great goodness we have never lacked, and may we not lack food forever, for the sake of His great Name. For He is Almighty, Who nourishes and sustains all, and does good to all, and prepares food for all His creatures that He has created. Blessed are You, Hashem, Who nourishes all.

We thank You, Hashem our God, because You have given us as a heritage to our forefathers a desirable, good, and spacious land; and because You brought us out, Hashem our God, from the land of Egypt, and redeemed us from the house of bondage; and for Your covenant that You sealed in our flesh; and for Your Torah that You taught

בָּרוּךְ אַתָּה יְיָ אֱלֹהֵינוּ מֶלֶךְ הָעוֹלָם, הַזָּן אֶת הָעוֹלָם כֻּלּוֹ בְּטוּבוֹ בְּחֵן בְּחֶסֶד וּבְרַחֲמִים, הוּא נוֹתֵן לֶחֶם לְכָל בָּשָׂר כִּי לְעוֹלָם חַסְדּוֹ, וּבְטוּבוֹ הַגָּדוֹל תָּמִיד לֹא חָסַר לָנוּ וְאַל יֶחְסַר לָנוּ מָזוֹן לְעוֹלָם וָעֶד, בַּעֲבוּר שְׁמוֹ הַגָּדוֹל, כִּי הוּא אֵל זָן וּמְפַרְנֵס לַכֹּל וּמֵטִיב לַכֹּל, וּמֵכִין מָזוֹן לְכָל בְּרִיּוֹתָיו אֲשֶׁר בָּרָא. בָּרוּךְ אַתָּה יְיָ, הַזָּן אֶת הַכֹּל:

נוֹדֶה לְךָ יְיָ אֱלֹהֵינוּ עַל שֶׁהִנְחַלְתָּ לַאֲבוֹתֵינוּ, אֶרֶץ חֶמְדָּה טוֹבָה וּרְחָבָה, וְעַל שֶׁהוֹצֵאתָנוּ יְיָ אֱלֹהֵינוּ מֵאֶרֶץ מִצְרַיִם, וּפְדִיתָנוּ מִבֵּית עֲבָדִים, וְעַל בְּרִיתְךָ שֶׁחָתַמְתָּ בִּבְשָׂרֵנוּ, וְעַל תּוֹרָתְךָ שֶׁלִּמַּדְתָּנוּ, וְעַל חֻקֶּיךָ שֶׁהוֹדַעְתָּנוּ, וְעַל

us; and for Your statutes that You made known to us; and for the life, favor, and kindness that You granted us; and for the provision of food with which You nourish and sustain us constantly, every day, in every season, and at every hour.

For everything, Hashem our God, we thank You and bless You. May Your Name be blessed by the mouth of all the living, constantly, forever, as it is written, "And you shall eat and be satisfied and you shall bless Hashem, Your God, for the good land that He has given you." Blessed are You, Hashem, for the land and for the food.

Please have compassion, Hashem our God, on Yisroel, Your people, on Yerushalayim Your city, on Zion the abode of Your glory, on the kingdom of the house of Dovid Your anointed, and on the great and holy House upon which Your Name is called. Our God,

חַיִּים חֵן וָחֶסֶד שֶׁחוֹנַנְתָּנוּ, וְעַל אֲכִילַת מָזוֹן שָׁאַתָּה זָן וּמְפַרְנֵס אוֹתָנוּ תָּמִיד, בְּכָל יוֹם וּבְכָל עֵת וּבְכָל שָׁעָה:

וְעַל הַכֹּל יְיָ אֱלֹהֵינוּ אֲנַחְנוּ מוֹדִים לָךְ, וּמְבָרְכִים אוֹתָךְ, יִתְבָּרַךְ שִׁמְךָ בְּפִי כָל חַי תָּמִיד לְעוֹלָם וָעֶד. כַּכָּתוּב. וְאָכַלְתָּ וְשָׂבָעְתָּ, וּבֵרַכְתָּ אֶת יְהֹוָה אֱלֹהֶיךָ עַל הָאָרֶץ הַטֹּבָה אֲשֶׁר נָתַן לָךְ. בָּרוּךְ אַתָּה יְיָ עַל הָאָרֶץ וְעַל הַמָּזוֹן:

רַחֵם נָא יְיָ אֱלֹהֵינוּ, עַל יִשְׂרָאֵל עַמֶּךָ, וְעַל יְרוּשָׁלַיִם עִירֶךָ, וְעַל צִיּוֹן מִשְׁכַּן כְּבוֹדֶךָ, וְעַל מַלְכוּת בֵּית דָּוִד מְשִׁיחֶךָ, וְעַל הַבַּיִת הַגָּדוֹל וְהַקָּדוֹשׁ שֶׁנִּקְרָא שִׁמְךָ עָלָיו. אֱלֹהֵינוּ אָבִינוּ, רְעֵנוּ זוֹנֵנוּ פַּרְנְסֵנוּ

Our Father, tend us, nourish us, sustain us, support us, relieve us, and grant us relief, Hashem our God, speedily from all our troubles. And please, Hashem our God, let us not be in need of the gifts of human hands, nor of their loans, but only of Your hand which is full, open, holy, and generous, so that we may not be shamed, or humiliated forever and ever.

וְכַלְכְּלֵנוּ וְהַרְוִיחֵנוּ, וְהַרְוַח לָנוּ יְיָ אֱלֹהֵינוּ מְהֵרָה מִכָּל צָרוֹתֵינוּ. וְנָא אַל תַּצְרִיכֵנוּ יְיָ אֱלֹהֵינוּ לֹא לִידֵי מַתְּנַת בָּשָׂר וָדָם, וְלֹא לִידֵי הַלְוָאָתָם, כִּי אִם לְיָדְךָ הַמְּלֵאָה הַפְּתוּחָה הַקְּדוֹשָׁה וְהָרְחָבָה, שֶׁלֹּא נֵבוֹשׁ וְלֹא נִכָּלֵם לְעוֹלָם וָעֶד:

On Shabbos

May it please You to strengthen us, Hashem our God, by Your commandments, and by the commandment of the seventh day, this great and holy Shabbos. For this day is great and holy before You, to refrain from work on it, and to rest on it, with love, as ordained by Your will. And by Your will, grant us rest, Hashem our God, that there be no distress, grief, or sighing, on the day of our rest. And show us, Hashem our God, the consolation of Zion Your city, and the rebuilding of Yerushalayim, the city of Your holiness, for You are the Master of salvations, and the Master of consolations.

רְצֵה וְהַחֲלִיצֵנוּ יְיָ אֱלֹהֵינוּ בְּמִצְוֹתֶיךָ, וּבְמִצְוַת יוֹם הַשְּׁבִיעִי הַשַּׁבָּת הַגָּדוֹל וְהַקָּדוֹשׁ הַזֶּה, כִּי יוֹם זֶה גָּדוֹל וְקָדוֹשׁ הוּא לְפָנֶיךָ, לִשְׁבָּת בּוֹ וְלָנוּחַ בּוֹ בְּאַהֲבָה כְּמִצְוַת רְצוֹנֶךָ, וּבִרְצוֹנְךָ הָנִיחַ לָנוּ יְיָ אֱלֹהֵינוּ שֶׁלֹּא תְהֵא צָרָה וְיָגוֹן וַאֲנָחָה בְּיוֹם מְנוּחָתֵנוּ, וְהַרְאֵנוּ יְיָ אֱלֹהֵינוּ בְּנֶחָמַת צִיּוֹן עִירֶךָ וּבְבִנְיַן יְרוּשָׁלַיִם עִיר קָדְשֶׁךָ, כִּי אַתָּה הוּא בַּעַל הַיְשׁוּעוֹת וּבַעַל הַנֶּחָמוֹת:

Our God, and God of our forefathers, may there rise, come, reach, and appear, be favored, heard, considered and remembered, our remembrance and consideration, the remembrance of our forefathers, the remembrance of Mashiach the son of Dovid Your servant, the remembrance of Yerushalayim city of Your holiness, and the remembrance of Your entire people the house of Yisroel, before You, for deliverance, for well-being, for favor, kindness and compassion, for life and peace on this day, the Festival of Matzos. Remember us, Hashem our God, on this day, for well-being; consider us on it for blessing; and save us on it for life. And in the promise of salvation and compassion, spare and favor us, have compassion on us, and deliver us, for our eyes are turned to You, because You are the Almighty, Who is the gracious and compassionate King.

אֱלֹהֵינוּ וֵאלֹהֵי אֲבוֹתֵינוּ, יַעֲלֶה וְיָבֹא וְיַגִּיעַ וְיֵרָאֶה וְיֵרָצֶה וְיִשָּׁמַע וְיִפָּקֵד וְיִזָּכֵר זִכְרוֹנֵנוּ וּפִקְדוֹנֵנוּ, וְזִכְרוֹן אֲבוֹתֵינוּ, וְזִכְרוֹן מָשִׁיחַ בֶּן דָּוִד עַבְדֶּךָ, וְזִכְרוֹן יְרוּשָׁלַיִם עִיר קָדְשֶׁךָ, וְזִכְרוֹן כָּל עַמְּךָ בֵּית יִשְׂרָאֵל לְפָנֶיךָ, לִפְלֵיטָה לְטוֹבָה לְחֵן וּלְחֶסֶד וּלְרַחֲמִים לְחַיִּים וּלְשָׁלוֹם בְּיוֹם חַג הַמַּצּוֹת הַזֶּה, זָכְרֵנוּ יְיָ אֱלֹהֵינוּ בּוֹ לְטוֹבָה, וּפָקְדֵנוּ בּוֹ לִבְרָכָה, וְהוֹשִׁיעֵנוּ בּוֹ לְחַיִּים, וּבִדְבַר יְשׁוּעָה וְרַחֲמִים חוּס וְחָנֵּנוּ וְרַחֵם עָלֵינוּ וְהוֹשִׁיעֵנוּ, כִּי אֵלֶיךָ עֵינֵינוּ, כִּי אֵל מֶלֶךְ חַנּוּן וְרַחוּם אָתָּה:

And rebuild Yerushalayim, the holy city, speedily in our days. Blessed are You, Who in His mercy rebuilds Yerushalayim. Amen.

וּבְנֵה יְרוּשָׁלַיִם עִיר הַקֹּדֶשׁ בִּמְהֵרָה בְיָמֵינוּ. בָּרוּךְ אַתָּה יְיָ בּוֹנֵה בְרַחֲמָיו יְרוּשָׁלָיִם, אָמֵן:

Blessed are You, Hashem our God, King of the universe, the Almighty, our Father, our King, our Mighty One, our Creator, our Redeemer, our Maker, our Holy One, the Holy One of Yaakov, our Shepherd, the Shepherd of Yisroel, the King Who is good and does good to all. For every single day He did good, does good, and will do good to us. He was benevolent to us, is benevolent to us, will be benevolent to us forever, with favor, kindness, compassion, relief, salvation, success, blessing, deliverance, consolation, sustenance, support, mercy, life, peace, and everything good. And of all good things may He never deprive us.

בָּרוּךְ אַתָּה יְיָ אֱלֹהֵינוּ מֶלֶךְ הָעוֹלָם, הָאֵל אָבִינוּ מַלְכֵּנוּ אַדִּירֵנוּ בּוֹרְאֵנוּ גּוֹאֲלֵנוּ יוֹצְרֵנוּ קְדוֹשֵׁנוּ קְדוֹשׁ יַעֲקֹב, רוֹעֵנוּ רוֹעֵה יִשְׂרָאֵל, הַמֶּלֶךְ הַטּוֹב וְהַמֵּטִיב לַכֹּל, שֶׁבְּכָל יוֹם וָיוֹם הוּא הֵטִיב הוּא מֵטִיב הוּא יֵיטִיב לָנוּ, הוּא גְמָלָנוּ הוּא גוֹמְלֵנוּ הוּא יִגְמְלֵנוּ לָעַד, לְחֵן וּלְחֶסֶד וּלְרַחֲמִים וּלְרֶוַח הַצָּלָה וְהַצְלָחָה, בְּרָכָה וִישׁוּעָה נֶחָמָה פַּרְנָסָה וְכַלְכָּלָה, וְרַחֲמִים וְחַיִּים וְשָׁלוֹם וְכָל טוֹב, וּמִכָּל טוּב לְעוֹלָם אַל יְחַסְּרֵנוּ:

Visitors add:

May it be God's will that this host will not be shamed or humiliated in this world or in the World to Come. May he have great success with all his possessions, and may his properties be successful and close to town. May no evil force have power over his endeavors, and may no matter of sin or iniquitous thought present itself to him, from now and forever.

יְהִי רָצוֹן שֶׁלֹּא יֵבוֹשׁ וְלֹא יִכָּלֵם בַּעַל הַבַּיִת הַזֶּה, לֹא בָּעוֹלָם הַזֶּה וְלֹא בָּעוֹלָם הַבָּא, וְיַצְלִיחַ בְּכָל נְכָסָיו, וְיִהְיוּ נְכָסָיו מֻצְלָחִים וּקְרוֹבִים לָעִיר, וְאַל יִשְׁלוֹט שָׂטָן בְּמַעֲשֵׂה יָדָיו, וְאַל יִזְדַּקֵּק לְפָנָיו שׁוּם דְּבַר הִרְהוּר חֵטְא וְעָוֹן מֵעַתָּה וְעַד עוֹלָם:

May the compassionate One reign over us forever and ever.

May the compassionate One be blessed in heaven and on earth.

May the compassionate One be praised for all generations, be glorified through us forever and for all eternity, and be honored through us for time everlasting.

May the compassionate One sustain us in honor.

May the compassionate One break the yoke of our exile from our necks, and lead us upright to our land.

May the compassionate One send us abundant blessing to this house, and upon this table at which we have eaten.

May the compassionate One send us *Eliyahu Hanavi* who is remembered for good, to announce to us good tidings, salvations, and consolations.

הָרַחֲמָן, הוּא יִמְלוֹךְ עָלֵינוּ לְעוֹלָם וָעֶד:

הָרַחֲמָן, הוּא יִתְבָּרַךְ בַּשָּׁמַיִם וּבָאָרֶץ:

הָרַחֲמָן, הוּא יִשְׁתַּבַּח לְדוֹר דּוֹרִים, וְיִתְפָּאַר בָּנוּ לָעַד וּלְנֵצַח נְצָחִים, וְיִתְהַדָּר בָּנוּ לָעַד וּלְעוֹלְמֵי עוֹלָמִים:

הָרַחֲמָן, הוּא יְפַרְנְסֵנוּ בְּכָבוֹד:

הָרַחֲמָן, הוּא יִשְׁבּוֹר עֹל גָּלוּתֵנוּ מֵעַל צַוָּארֵנוּ וְהוּא יוֹלִיכֵנוּ קוֹמְמִיּוּת לְאַרְצֵנוּ:

הָרַחֲמָן, הוּא יִשְׁלַח לָנוּ בְּרָכָה מְרֻבָּה בַּבַּיִת הַזֶּה, וְעַל שֻׁלְחָן זֶה שֶׁאָכַלְנוּ עָלָיו:

הָרַחֲמָן, הוּא יִשְׁלַח לָנוּ אֶת אֵלִיָּהוּ הַנָּבִיא זָכוּר לַטּוֹב וִיבַשֶּׂר לָנוּ בְּשׂוֹרוֹת טוֹבוֹת יְשׁוּעוֹת וְנֶחָמוֹת:

The Guidelines Haggadah

Each person should say the appropriate lines:

May the compassionate One bless the master of this house, and the lady of this house,

May the compassionate One bless my father my teacher, and my mother my teacher.

May the compassionate One bless me, my wife/husband, my children and all that is mine.

Us, and all that is ours, just as our forefathers, Avraham, Yitzchak, and Yaakov, were blessed in everything, from everything, with everything. So may He bless us all together with a perfect blessing, and let us say, Amen.

On high, may there be invoked upon them and upon us the merit to safeguard peace. And may we receive a blessing from Hashem and kindness from the God of our salvation. And may we find favor and understanding in the eyes of God and man.

הָרַחֲמָן, הוּא יְבָרֵךְ אֶת בַּעַל הַבַּיִת הַזֶּה וְאֶת בַּעֲלַת הַבַּיִת הַזֶּה,

הָרַחֲמָן, הוּא יְבָרֵךְ אֶת אָבִי מוֹרִי וְאֶת אִמִּי מוֹרָתִי,

הָרַחֲמָן, הוּא יְבָרֵךְ אוֹתִי וְאֶת אִשְׁתִּי/ בַּעְלִי וְאֶת זַרְעִי וְאֶת כָּל אֲשֶׁר לִי,

אוֹתָנוּ וְאֶת כָּל אֲשֶׁר לָנוּ, כְּמוֹ שֶׁנִּתְבָּרְכוּ אֲבוֹתֵינוּ אַבְרָהָם יִצְחָק וְיַעֲקֹב בַּכֹּל מִכֹּל כֹּל, כֵּן יְבָרֵךְ אוֹתָנוּ כֻּלָּנוּ יַחַד, בִּבְרָכָה שְׁלֵמָה, וְנֹאמַר אָמֵן:

בַּמָּרוֹם יְלַמְּדוּ עֲלֵיהֶם וְעָלֵינוּ זְכוּת שֶׁתְּהֵא לְמִשְׁמֶרֶת שָׁלוֹם, וְנִשָּׂא בְרָכָה מֵאֵת יְיָ וּצְדָקָה מֵאֱלֹהֵי יִשְׁעֵנוּ, וְנִמְצָא חֵן וְשֵׂכֶל טוֹב בְּעֵינֵי אֱלֹהִים וְאָדָם:

On Shabbos:

May the compassionate One let us inherit the day that will be completely Shabbos and rest for eternal life.

הָרַחֲמָן, הוּא יַנְחִילֵנוּ יוֹם שֶׁכֻּלוֹ שַׁבָּת וּמְנוּחָה לְחַיֵּי הָעוֹלָמִים:

May the compassionate One let us inherit the day that is completely good. The day that is everlasting, the day when the righteous will sit with crowns on their heads and enjoy the light of the *Shechina*. May our portion be with them!

May the compassionate One make us worthy of the days of *Mashiach*, and the life of the World to Come.

הָרַחֲמָן הוּא יַנְחִילֵנוּ יוֹם שֶׁכֻּלוֹ טוֹב. יוֹם שֶׁכֻּלוֹ אָרֹךְ, יוֹם שֶׁצַּדִּיקִים יוֹשְׁבִים וְעַטְרוֹתֵיהֶם בְּרָאשֵׁיהֶם וְנֶהֱנִים מִזִּיו הַשְּׁכִינָה, וִיהִי חֶלְקֵנוּ עִמָּהֶם: הָרַחֲמָן, הוּא יְזַכֵּנוּ לִימוֹת הַמָּשִׁיחַ וּלְחַיֵּי הָעוֹלָם הַבָּא:

He Who is a tower of salvations to His king and does kindness to His anointed, to Dovid and his descendants forever. He Who makes peace in His high heavens, may He make peace upon us and upon all Yisroel, and say, Amen.

מִגְדּוֹל יְשׁוּעוֹת מַלְכּוֹ וְעֹשֶׂה חֶסֶד לִמְשִׁיחוֹ לְדָוִד וּלְזַרְעוֹ עַד עוֹלָם: עֹשֶׂה שָׁלוֹם בִּמְרוֹמָיו הוּא יַעֲשֶׂה שָׁלוֹם עָלֵינוּ וְעַל כָּל יִשְׂרָאֵל, וְאִמְרוּ אָמֵן:

The Guidelines Haggadah

Fear Hashem, you His holy ones, for there is no deprivation for those who fear Him. Young lions may feel want and hunger, but those who seek Hashem will not lack any good thing. Thank Hashem for He is good, for His kindness endures forever. You open Your hand and satisfy the desire of every living being. Blessed is the man who trusts in Hashem, then Hashem will be his security. I was young and also have aged, and I have not seen a righteous man forsaken and his children begging for bread. Hashem will give strength to His people, Hashem will bless His people with peace.

יְראוּ אֶת יְהֹוָה קְדֹשָׁיו, כִּי אֵין מַחְסוֹר לִירֵאָיו: כְּפִירִים רָשׁוּ וְרָעֵבוּ, וְדֹרְשֵׁי יְהֹוָה לֹא יַחְסְרוּ כָל טוֹב: הוֹדוּ לַיהֹוָה כִּי טוֹב, כִּי לְעוֹלָם חַסְדּוֹ: פּוֹתֵחַ אֶת יָדֶךָ, וּמַשְׂבִּיעַ לְכָל חַי רָצוֹן: בָּרוּךְ הַגֶּבֶר אֲשֶׁר יִבְטַח בַּיהֹוָה, וְהָיָה יְהֹוָה מִבְטַחוֹ: נַעַר הָיִיתִי גַּם זָקַנְתִּי, וְלֹא רָאִיתִי צַדִּיק נֶעֱזָב וְזַרְעוֹ מְבַקֶּשׁ לָחֶם: יְהֹוָה עֹז לְעַמּוֹ יִתֵּן, יְהֹוָה יְבָרֵךְ אֶת עַמּוֹ בַשָּׁלוֹם:

> *Hold the cup of wine, if not already doing so.*
> *Before drinking the wine, one should think that he is about to fulfill*
> *the Rabbinic mitzvah of drinking the third of the four cups of wine.*
> *A man should recline when drinking the wine. If he forgot to recline,*
> *he should not drink another cup.*

Blessed are You, Hashem our God, King of the universe, Who creates the fruit of the vine.

בָּרוּךְ אַתָּה יְיָ אֱלֹהֵינוּ מֶלֶךְ הָעוֹלָם, בּוֹרֵא פְּרִי הַגָּפֶן:

362. If a person forgot to say *Ya'aleh Ve'yavo* (or *retzei* on Shabbos) and already began the fourth *b'racha* (*Ha'eil Avinu*), he must repeat *bensching* before drinking the wine.

363. If he realized his omission after drinking the wine, he should repeat *bensching* with another cup of wine. However, the wine should not be drunk after *bensching*, but should be left and drunk for the fourth cup.

364. After drinking the third cup, the cups are refilled, and an extra cup is filled, known as the cup of Eliyahu Hanavi. (Some have the custom to fill this cup before *bensching*.)

365. The custom is for the leader of the Seder to fill the cup of Eliyahu Hanavi. It should be a large and especially beautiful cup.

The Guidelines Haggadah

366. Many have the custom to leave the cup of Eliyahu Hanavi covered on the table overnight and use it for Kiddush on Yom Tov morning. Others pour it back into the bottle.

367. The door is opened and the paragraph שפוך חמתך is recited. (Some have the custom to fill the fourth cup after this paragraph.)

368. The door is opened for שפוך חמתך in order to remember that Hashem protects the Jewish people on this night. In the merit of our faith in Hashem, we hope to be worthy to witness the coming of *Mashiach* and the punishment of the nations who deny the existence of Hashem.

369. The custom is to recite שפוך חמתך standing.

Pour Your wrath upon the nations that do not know You, and upon the kingdoms that do not call upon Your Name. For they have devoured Yaakov, and destroyed His dwelling. Pour Your anger upon them and let Your fierce wrath overtake them. Pursue them with wrath and destroy them from beneath the heavens of Hashem.

שְׁפֹךְ חֲמָתְךָ אֶל הַגּוֹיִם אֲשֶׁר לֹא יְדָעוּךָ וְעַל מַמְלָכוֹת אֲשֶׁר בְּשִׁמְךָ לֹא קָרָאוּ: כִּי אָכַל אֶת יַעֲקֹב וְאֶת נָוֵהוּ הֵשַׁמּוּ: שְׁפָךְ עֲלֵיהֶם זַעְמֶךָ וַחֲרוֹן אַפְּךָ יַשִּׂיגֵם: תִּרְדֹּף בְּאַף וְתַשְׁמִידֵם מִתַּחַת שְׁמֵי יְהוָה:

הַלֵּל

Hallel

Recite the Hallel

370. Before reciting Hallel, one should think that he is about to fulfill the Rabbinic mitzvah of reciting Hallel.

371. Women are obligated to remain at the Seder for Hallel and the fourth cup of wine.

372. Children (aged five or six) should be encouraged to do so if possible.

373. Some have the custom to leave matza on the table during Hallel.

374. If possible, it is preferable for everyone to hold the cup of wine during Hallel until the wine is drunk. When reaching the verse, "'I will lift the cup of deliverance'", the cup should be raised slightly.

375. One should not recline during Hallel. Rather, one should sit upright with awe and respect.

376. Ideally, one should not talk about anything unnecessary from this point until after drinking the fourth cup of wine.

The Guidelines Haggadah

Not for our sake, Hashem, not for our sake, but for the sake of Your Name, give honor because of Your kindness and Your truth. Why should the nations say, "Where now is their God?" But our God is in heaven; He does whatever He pleases. Their idols are silver and gold, the work of human hands. They have a mouth but cannot speak, they have eyes but cannot see. They have ears but cannot hear, they have a nose but cannot smell. Their hands cannot feel, their feet cannot walk; they cannot utter a sound with their throat. Those who make them, shall become like them, [and also] whoever trusts in them. Yisroel, trust in Hashem, He is their help and their shield. House of Aharon trust in Hashem, He is their help and their shield. You who fear Hashem trust in Hashem, He is their help and their shield.

Hashem, Who has been mindful of us, will bless - He will bless the house of Yisroel; He will bless the house of Aharon. He will bless

לֹא לָנוּ יְהֹוָה לֹא לָנוּ, כִּי לְשִׁמְךָ תֵּן כָּבוֹד עַל חַסְדְּךָ עַל אֲמִתֶּךָ: לָמָּה יֹאמְרוּ הַגּוֹיִם, אַיֵּה נָא אֱלֹהֵיהֶם: וֵאלֹהֵינוּ בַשָּׁמָיִם, כֹּל אֲשֶׁר חָפֵץ עָשָׂה: עֲצַבֵּיהֶם כֶּסֶף וְזָהָב, מַעֲשֵׂה יְדֵי אָדָם: פֶּה לָהֶם וְלֹא יְדַבֵּרוּ, עֵינַיִם לָהֶם וְלֹא יִרְאוּ: אָזְנַיִם לָהֶם וְלֹא יִשְׁמָעוּ, אַף לָהֶם וְלֹא יְרִיחוּן: יְדֵיהֶם וְלֹא יְמִישׁוּן רַגְלֵיהֶם וְלֹא יְהַלֵּכוּ, לֹא יֶהְגּוּ בִּגְרוֹנָם: כְּמוֹהֶם יִהְיוּ עֹשֵׂיהֶם, כֹּל אֲשֶׁר בֹּטֵחַ בָּהֶם: יִשְׂרָאֵל בְּטַח בַּיהוָה, עֶזְרָם וּמָגִנָּם הוּא: בֵּית אַהֲרֹן בִּטְחוּ בַיהוָה, עֶזְרָם וּמָגִנָּם הוּא: יִרְאֵי יְהֹוָה בִּטְחוּ בַיהוָה, עֶזְרָם וּמָגִנָּם הוּא:

יְהֹוָה זְכָרָנוּ יְבָרֵךְ, יְבָרֵךְ אֶת בֵּית יִשְׂרָאֵל, יְבָרֵךְ אֶת בֵּית אַהֲרֹן: יְבָרֵךְ יִרְאֵי

those who fear Hashem, the small with the great. May Hashem increase [His blessing] to you, to you and your children. You are blessed by Hashem, Creator of heaven and earth. The heavens belong to Hashem; the earth He has given to mankind. The dead do not praise Hashem; those who go down to the grave. But we will bless Hashem, from now and forever, Halleluyah.

I love Hashem, for He listens to my voice, my supplications. Because He turned His ear to me, I shall call [Him] throughout my days. I was gripped by pangs of death, and the confines of the grave came upon me; I faced trouble and sorrow. But I called upon the name of Hashem, "Please Hashem, deliver my soul!" Hashem is gracious and righteous, and our God is merciful. Hashem protects the simple; I was brought low but He delivered me. My soul, return to your rest; for Hashem has rewarded you bountifully. For You delivered my soul from

יְהֹוָה, הַקְּטַנִּים עִם הַגְּדֹלִים: יֹסֵף יְהֹוָה עֲלֵיכֶם, עֲלֵיכֶם וְעַל בְּנֵיכֶם: בְּרוּכִים אַתֶּם לַיהֹוָה, עֹשֵׂה שָׁמַיִם וָאָרֶץ: הַשָּׁמַיִם שָׁמַיִם לַיהֹוָה, וְהָאָרֶץ נָתַן לִבְנֵי אָדָם: לֹא הַמֵּתִים יְהַלְלוּ יָהּ, וְלֹא כָּל יֹרְדֵי דוּמָה: וַאֲנַחְנוּ נְבָרֵךְ יָהּ, מֵעַתָּה וְעַד עוֹלָם, הַלְלוּיָהּ:

אָהַבְתִּי כִּי יִשְׁמַע יְהֹוָה, אֶת קוֹלִי תַּחֲנוּנָי: כִּי הִטָּה אָזְנוֹ לִי, וּבְיָמַי אֶקְרָא: אֲפָפוּנִי חֶבְלֵי מָוֶת, וּמְצָרֵי שְׁאוֹל מְצָאוּנִי, צָרָה וְיָגוֹן אֶמְצָא: וּבְשֵׁם יְהֹוָה אֶקְרָא, אָנָּה יְהֹוָה מַלְּטָה נַפְשִׁי: חַנּוּן יְהֹוָה וְצַדִּיק, וֵאלֹהֵינוּ מְרַחֵם: שֹׁמֵר פְּתָאִים יְהֹוָה, דַּלּוֹתִי וְלִי יְהוֹשִׁיעַ: שׁוּבִי נַפְשִׁי לִמְנוּחָיְכִי, כִּי יְהֹוָה גָּמַל עָלָיְכִי: כִּי חִלַּצְתָּ נַפְשִׁי מִמָּוֶת, אֶת עֵינִי מִן דִּמְעָה אֶת רַגְלִי מִדֶּחִי:

death, my eye from tears, my foot from stumbling. I shall walk before Hashem in the lands of the living. I had faith, although I said, "I suffer greatly". I said hastily, "All men are deceitful".

How can I repay Hashem for all the bounties He has bestowed upon me?

If one is holding the wine, he should raise it slightly when saying the following verse.

I will lift the cup of deliverance, and I will call in the name of Hashem. I will fulfill my vows to Hashem, in the presence of His entire people. The death of His pious ones is harsh in the eyes of Hashem. Please Hashem, for I am Your servant; I am Your servant the son of Your handmaid, You have untied my bonds. I will sacrifice an offering of thanks to You, and I will call in the Name of Hashem. I will fulfill my vows to Hashem, in the presence of His entire people. In the courtyards of the house of Hashem, in the midst of Yerushalayim, Halleluyah.

אֶתְהַלֵּךְ לִפְנֵי יְהֹוָה, בְּאַרְצוֹת הַחַיִּים: הֶאֱמַנְתִּי כִּי אֲדַבֵּר, אֲנִי עָנִיתִי מְאֹד: אֲנִי אָמַרְתִּי בְחָפְזִי, כָּל הָאָדָם כֹּזֵב:

מָה אָשִׁיב לַיהֹוָה, כָּל תַּגְמוּלוֹהִי עָלָי:

כּוֹס יְשׁוּעוֹת אֶשָּׂא, וּבְשֵׁם יְהֹוָה אֶקְרָא: נְדָרַי לַיהֹוָה אֲשַׁלֵּם, נֶגְדָה נָּא לְכָל עַמּוֹ: יָקָר בְּעֵינֵי יְהֹוָה, הַמָּוְתָה לַחֲסִידָיו: אָנָּה יְהֹוָה כִּי אֲנִי עַבְדֶּךָ, אֲנִי עַבְדְּךָ בֶּן אֲמָתֶךָ, פִּתַּחְתָּ לְמוֹסֵרָי: לְךָ אֶזְבַּח זֶבַח תּוֹדָה וּבְשֵׁם יְהֹוָה אֶקְרָא: נְדָרַי לַיהֹוָה אֲשַׁלֵּם, נֶגְדָה נָּא לְכָל עַמּוֹ: בְּחַצְרוֹת בֵּית יְהֹוָה, בְּתוֹכֵכִי יְרוּשָׁלָיִם, הַלְלוּיָהּ:

Praise Hashem all nations, extol Him all peoples! For His kindness has overwhelmed us, and Hashem"s truth is eternal, Halleluyah!

הַלְלוּ אֶת יְהֹוָה כָּל גּוֹיִם, שַׁבְּחוּהוּ כָּל הָאֻמִּים: כִּי גָבַר עָלֵינוּ חַסְדּוֹ, וֶאֱמֶת יְהֹוָה לְעוֹלָם, הַלְלוּיָהּ:

> *If there are at least three people present, including one's wife and children, the verses of הודו and אנא should be said responsively, as is done in shul. The leader of the Seder should recite these verses and the others should respond.*

Thank Hashem for He is good,
     for His kindness endures forever.

הוֹדוּ לַיהֹוָה כִּי טוֹב   כִּי לְעוֹלָם חַסְדּוֹ:

Let Yisroel say so,
     for His kindness endures forever.

יֹאמַר נָא יִשְׂרָאֵל   כִּי לְעוֹלָם חַסְדּוֹ:

Let the house of Aharon say so,
     for His kindness endures forever.

יֹאמְרוּ נָא בֵית אַהֲרֹן   כִּי לְעוֹלָם חַסְדּוֹ:

Let those who fear Hashem say so,
     for His kindness endures forever.

יֹאמְרוּ נָא יִרְאֵי יְהֹוָה   כִּי לְעוֹלָם חַסְדּוֹ:

From the straits I called Hashem; He answered me with His expansiveness. Hashem is with me, I will not fear - what can man do to me? Hashem is with me and with my helpers, and I will face my enemies. It is better to take shelter in Hashem, than to rely on man. It is better to take shelter in

מִן הַמֵּצַר קָרָאתִי יָּהּ, עָנָנִי בַמֶּרְחָב יָהּ: יְהֹוָה לִי לֹא אִירָא, מַה יַּעֲשֶׂה לִי אָדָם: יְהֹוָה לִי בְּעֹזְרָי, וַאֲנִי אֶרְאֶה בְשֹׂנְאָי: טוֹב לַחֲסוֹת בַּיהֹוָה, מִבְּטֹחַ בָּאָדָם: טוֹב לַחֲסוֹת בַּיהֹוָה, מִבְּטֹחַ בִּנְדִיבִים: כָּל גּוֹיִם

Hashem than to rely on nobles. All nations surround me; in the Name of Hashem I will cut them down. They truly surround me; in the Name of Hashem I will cut them down. They surround me like bees, they will be consumed like thorns on fire; in the Name of Hashem I will cut them down. You [enemies] pushed me to knock me down, but Hashem helped me. Hashem is my strength and my praise and this was my salvation. The sound of rejoicing and salvation is in the tents of the righteous. Hashem"s right hand does valiantly, Hashem"s right hand is triumphant, Hashem"s right hand does valiantly. I shall not die but I shall live and relate the deeds of Hashem. Hashem afflicted me heavily, but did not let me die. Open for me the gates of righteousness, I will enter them and thank Hashem. This is the gate of Hashem, the righteous shall enter it. I thank You for You answered me, and You have been my salvation. I thank You for You answered me, and You have been my salvation. The stone that the builders rejected became the cornerstone. The stone that the builders rejected became

סְבָבוּנִי, בְּשֵׁם יְהֹוָה כִּי אֲמִילַם: סַבּוּנִי גַם סְבָבוּנִי, בְּשֵׁם יְהֹוָה כִּי אֲמִילַם: סַבּוּנִי כִדְבוֹרִים דֹּעֲכוּ כְּאֵשׁ קוֹצִים, בְּשֵׁם יְהֹוָה כִּי אֲמִילַם: דָּחֹה דְחִיתַנִי לִנְפֹּל, וַיהֹוָה עֲזָרָנִי: עָזִּי וְזִמְרָת יָה, וַיְהִי לִי לִישׁוּעָה: קוֹל רִנָּה וִישׁוּעָה בְּאָהֳלֵי צַדִּיקִים, יְמִין יְהֹוָה עֹשָׂה חָיִל: יְמִין יְהֹוָה רוֹמֵמָה, יְמִין יְהֹוָה עֹשָׂה חָיִל: לֹא אָמוּת כִּי אֶחְיֶה, וַאֲסַפֵּר מַעֲשֵׂי יָה: יַסֹּר יִסְּרַנִי יָּה, וְלַמָּוֶת לֹא נְתָנָנִי: פִּתְחוּ לִי שַׁעֲרֵי צֶדֶק, אָבֹא בָם אוֹדֶה יָהּ: זֶה הַשַּׁעַר לַיהֹוָה, צַדִּיקִים יָבֹאוּ בוֹ:

אוֹדְךָ כִּי עֲנִיתָנִי, וַתְּהִי לִי לִישׁוּעָה: אוֹדְךָ כִּי עֲנִיתָנִי, וַתְּהִי לִי לִישׁוּעָה: אֶבֶן מָאֲסוּ הַבּוֹנִים, הָיְתָה לְרֹאשׁ פִּנָּה: אֶבֶן מָאֲסוּ הַבּוֹנִים, הָיְתָה לְרֹאשׁ פִּנָּה: מֵאֵת יְהֹוָה הָיְתָה זֹּאת, הִיא נִפְלָאת

the cornerstone. This came from Hashem; it is wondrous in our eyes. This came from Hashem; it is wondrous in our eyes. This day was made by Hashem, let us rejoice and be happy in Him. This day was made by Hashem, let us rejoice and be happy in Him.

Please Hashem, save us!

Please Hashem, save us!

Please Hashem, grant us success!

Please Hashem, grant us success!

Blessed is he who comes in the Name of Hashem; we bless you from the house of Hashem. Blessed is he who comes in the Name of Hashem; we bless you from the house of Hashem. Hashem is Almighty, He gave us light; bind the festival offering with ropes [until they are brought] to the corners of the altar. Hashem is Almighty, He gave us light; bind the festival offering with ropes [until they are brought] to the corners of the altar. You are my Almighty and I will thank You; my God, I will exalt

בְּעֵינֵינוּ: מֵאֵת יְהֹוָה הָיְתָה זֹּאת, הִיא נִפְלָאת בְּעֵינֵינוּ: זֶה הַיּוֹם עָשָׂה יְהֹוָה, נָגִילָה וְנִשְׂמְחָה בוֹ: זֶה הַיּוֹם עָשָׂה יְהֹוָה, נָגִילָה וְנִשְׂמְחָה בוֹ:

אָנָּא יְהֹוָה הוֹשִׁיעָה נָּא:

אָנָּא יְהֹוָה הוֹשִׁיעָה נָּא:

אָנָּא יְהֹוָה הַצְלִיחָה נָּא:

אָנָּא יְהֹוָה הַצְלִיחָה נָּא:

בָּרוּךְ הַבָּא בְּשֵׁם יְהֹוָה, בֵּרַכְנוּכֶם מִבֵּית יְהֹוָה: בָּרוּךְ הַבָּא בְּשֵׁם יְהֹוָה, בֵּרַכְנוּכֶם מִבֵּית יְהֹוָה: אֵל יְהֹוָה וַיָּאֶר לָנוּ, אִסְרוּ חַג בַּעֲבֹתִים עַד קַרְנוֹת הַמִּזְבֵּחַ: אֵל יְהֹוָה וַיָּאֶר לָנוּ, אִסְרוּ חַג בַּעֲבֹתִים עַד קַרְנוֹת הַמִּזְבֵּחַ: אֵלִי אַתָּה וְאוֹדֶךָּ, אֱלֹהַי אֲרוֹמְמֶךָּ: אֵלִי

The Guidelines Haggadah

You. You are my Almighty and I will thank You; my God, I will exalt You.

Thank Hashem for He is good, for His kindness endures forever. Thank Hashem for He is good, for His kindness endures forever.

אַתָּה וְאוֹדֶךָּ, אֱלֹהַי אֲרוֹמְמֶךָּ:
הוֹדוּ לַיהוָה כִּי טוֹב, כִּי לְעוֹלָם חַסְדּוֹ:
הוֹדוּ לַיהוָה כִּי טוֹב, כִּי לְעוֹלָם חַסְדּוֹ:

377. There are different customs about when to say the paragraph יהללוך. The main Ashkenaz custom is to recite it at this point but without the concluding b'racha. The paragraph ישתבח is concluded with the regular conclusion of Hallel, i.e. מלך מהולל בתשבחות. Some have the

custom to conclude ישתבח in the same way that it is said during *Shacharis*.

378. If one mistakenly concluded יהללוך with its b'racha, he should continue as usual, but the paragraph of ישתבח should not be concluded with a b'racha (i.e. stop before the word ברוך).

All Your works shall praise You, Hashem our God; and Your pious ones, the righteous, who do Your will, and Your entire nation, the house of Yisroel, will joyfully thank, bless, praise, glorify, exalt, extol, sanctify, and crown Your Name, our King. For it is fitting to give thanks and proper to sing praises to Your Name, because You are God from this world to the next world.

יְהַלְלוּךָ יְיָ אֱלֹהֵינוּ כָּל מַעֲשֶׂיךָ, וַחֲסִידֶיךָ צַדִּיקִים עוֹשֵׂי רְצוֹנֶךָ, וְכָל עַמְּךָ בֵּית יִשְׂרָאֵל, בְּרִנָּה יוֹדוּ וִיבָרְכוּ וִישַׁבְּחוּ וִיפָאֲרוּ וִירוֹמְמוּ וְיַעֲרִיצוּ וְיַקְדִּישׁוּ וְיַמְלִיכוּ אֶת שִׁמְךָ מַלְכֵּנוּ, כִּי לְךָ טוֹב לְהוֹדוֹת וּלְשִׁמְךָ נָאֶה לְזַמֵּר, כִּי מֵעוֹלָם וְעַד עוֹלָם אַתָּה אֵל:

124

Thank Hashem for He is good, for His kindness endures forever.	כִּי לְעוֹלָם חַסְדּוֹ:	**הוֹדוּ** לַיהוָה כִּי טוֹב
Thank the God of angels, for His kindness endures forever.	כִּי לְעוֹלָם חַסְדּוֹ:	הוֹדוּ לֵאלֹהֵי הָאֱלֹהִים
Thank the Master of masters, for His kindness endures forever.	כִּי לְעוֹלָם חַסְדּוֹ:	הוֹדוּ לַאֲדֹנֵי הָאֲדֹנִים
Who alone performs great wonders, for His kindness endures forever.	לְעֹשֵׂה נִפְלָאוֹת גְּדֹלוֹת לְבַדּוֹ כִּי לְעוֹלָם חַסְדּוֹ:	
He Who makes the heavens with understanding, for His kindness endures forever.	כִּי לְעוֹלָם חַסְדּוֹ:	לְעֹשֵׂה הַשָּׁמַיִם בִּתְבוּנָה
He Who spreads the earth upon the waters, for His kindness endures forever.	כִּי לְעוֹלָם חַסְדּוֹ:	לְרֹקַע הָאָרֶץ עַל הַמָּיִם
He Who makes the great luminaries, for His kindness endures forever.	כִּי לְעוֹלָם חַסְדּוֹ:	לְעֹשֵׂה אוֹרִים גְּדֹלִים
The sun to rule by day, for His kindness endures forever.	אֶת הַשֶּׁמֶשׁ לְמֶמְשֶׁלֶת בַּיּוֹם כִּי לְעוֹלָם חַסְדּוֹ:	
The moon and stars to rule by night, for His kindness endures forever.	אֶת הַיָּרֵחַ וְכוֹכָבִים לְמֶמְשְׁלוֹת בַּלָּיְלָה כִּי לְעוֹלָם חַסְדּוֹ:	
He Who struck Egypt with their firstborn, for His kindness endures forever.	כִּי לְעוֹלָם חַסְדּוֹ:	לְמַכֵּה מִצְרַיִם בִּבְכוֹרֵיהֶם
And He took Yisroel out of their midst, for His kindness endures forever.	כִּי לְעוֹלָם חַסְדּוֹ:	וַיּוֹצֵא יִשְׂרָאֵל מִתּוֹכָם
With a strong hand and outstreched arm, for His kindness endures forever.	כִּי לְעוֹלָם חַסְדּוֹ:	בְּיָד חֲזָקָה וּבִזְרוֹעַ נְטוּיָה
He Who parted the Sea of Reeds into parts, for His kindness endures forever.	כִּי לְעוֹלָם חַסְדּוֹ:	לְגֹזֵר יַם סוּף לִגְזָרִים

The Guidelines Haggadah

And brought Yisroel through it, for His kindness endures forever.	וְהֶעֱבִיר יִשְׂרָאֵל בְּתוֹכוֹ כִּי לְעוֹלָם חַסְדּוֹ:
And threw Pharoah and his army into the Sea of Reeds, for His kindness endures forever.	וְנִעֵר פַּרְעֹה וְחֵילוֹ בְיַם סוּף כִּי לְעוֹלָם חַסְדּוֹ:
He Who led His people through the wilderness, for His kindness endures forever.	לְמוֹלִיךְ עַמּוֹ בַּמִּדְבָּר כִּי לְעוֹלָם חַסְדּוֹ:
He Who smote great kings, for His kindness endures forever.	לְמַכֵּה מְלָכִים גְּדֹלִים כִּי לְעוֹלָם חַסְדּוֹ:
And He slew mighty kings, for His kindness endures forever.	וַיַּהֲרֹג מְלָכִים אַדִּירִים כִּי לְעוֹלָם חַסְדּוֹ:
Sichon, king of the Emorites, for His kindness endures forever.	לְסִיחוֹן מֶלֶךְ הָאֱמֹרִי כִּי לְעוֹלָם חַסְדּוֹ:
And Og, king of the Bashan, for His kindness endures forever.	וּלְעוֹג מֶלֶךְ הַבָּשָׁן כִּי לְעוֹלָם חַסְדּוֹ:
And gave their land as an inheritance, for His kindness endures forever.	וְנָתַן אַרְצָם לְנַחֲלָה כִּי לְעוֹלָם חַסְדּוֹ:
An inheritance for Yisroel His servant, for His kindness endures forever.	נַחֲלָה לְיִשְׂרָאֵל עַבְדּוֹ כִּי לְעוֹלָם חַסְדּוֹ:
In our lowliness He remembered us, for His kindness endures forever.	שֶׁבְּשִׁפְלֵנוּ זָכַר לָנוּ כִּי לְעוֹלָם חַסְדּוֹ:
And delivered us from our oppressors, for His kindness endures forever.	וַיִּפְרְקֵנוּ מִצָּרֵינוּ כִּי לְעוֹלָם חַסְדּוֹ:
He gives nourishment to all flesh, for His kindness endures forever.	נֹתֵן לֶחֶם לְכָל בָּשָׂר כִּי לְעוֹלָם חַסְדּוֹ:
Thank the Almighty of heaven, for His kindness endures forever.	הוֹדוּ לְאֵל הַשָּׁמָיִם כִּי לְעוֹלָם חַסְדּוֹ:

The soul of every living being shall bless Your Name, Hashem our God, and the spirit of all flesh shall continually glorify and exalt Your rememberance, our King. From this world to the next world You are Almighty, and besides You we have no king, redeemer, saviour, liberator, rescuer, sustainer, and merciful One; in all times of trouble and distress, we have no king but You. God of the first and last [generations], God of all creatures, Master of all generations, Who is extolled with a multitude of praises, Who guides the world with kindness and His creatures with mercy. Hashem neither slumbers nor sleeps, He awakens the sleepers, and arouses the slumberers. He gives speech to the mute, releases the imprisoned, supports the falling, and straightens the bent; to You alone we give thanks. Were our mouths as full of song as the sea [is full of water], and our tongues as full of joyous song as its multitude of waves, and our lips as full of priase as the breadth of the heavens, and our eyes as

נִשְׁמַת כָּל חַי תְּבָרֵךְ אֶת שִׁמְךָ יְיָ
אֱלֹהֵינוּ, וְרוּחַ כָּל בָּשָׂר תְּפָאֵר וּתְרוֹמֵם
זִכְרְךָ מַלְכֵּנוּ תָּמִיד, מִן הָעוֹלָם וְעַד
הָעוֹלָם אַתָּה אֵל, וּמִבַּלְעָדֶיךָ אֵין לָנוּ
מֶלֶךְ גּוֹאֵל וּמוֹשִׁיעַ, פּוֹדֶה וּמַצִּיל וּמְפַרְנֵס
וּמְרַחֵם בְּכָל עֵת צָרָה וְצוּקָה, אֵין לָנוּ
מֶלֶךְ אֶלָּא אָתָּה. אֱלֹהֵי הָרִאשׁוֹנִים
וְהָאַחֲרוֹנִים, אֱלוֹהַּ כָּל בְּרִיּוֹת, אֲדוֹן
כָּל תּוֹלָדוֹת, הַמְהֻלָּל בְּרֹב הַתִּשְׁבָּחוֹת,
הַמְנַהֵג עוֹלָמוֹ בְּחֶסֶד וּבְרִיּוֹתָיו בְּרַחֲמִים.
וַיְיָ לֹא יָנוּם וְלֹא יִישָׁן, הַמְעוֹרֵר יְשֵׁנִים,
וְהַמֵּקִיץ נִרְדָּמִים, וְהַמֵּשִׂיחַ אִלְּמִים,
וְהַמַּתִּיר אֲסוּרִים, וְהַסּוֹמֵךְ נוֹפְלִים,
וְהַזּוֹקֵף כְּפוּפִים, לְךָ לְבַדְּךָ אֲנַחְנוּ מוֹדִים.
אִלּוּ פִינוּ מָלֵא שִׁירָה כַּיָּם, וּלְשׁוֹנֵנוּ רִנָּה
כַּהֲמוֹן גַּלָּיו, וְשִׂפְתוֹתֵינוּ שֶׁבַח כְּמֶרְחֲבֵי

radiant as the sun and the moon, and our hands outspread as eagles of the sky, and our feet swift as gazelles - we would never sufficiently thank You, Hashem our God and God of our fathers, and bless Your Name for even one thousandth of the billions and trillions of favors that You did for our forefathers and for us.

You redeemed us from Egypt, Hashem our God, and liberated us from the house of bondage. In famine You nourished us, and in times of plenty You sustained us. From the sword You saved us, and from plague You let us escape, and from severe and enduring illness you spared us. Until now Your mercy has helped us and Your kindness has not forsaken us - do not abandon us, Hashem our God, forever. Therefore, the limbs that You placed within us and the spirit and soul that You breathed into our nostrils and the tongue that You placed in our mouth - all of them will thank, bless, praise, glorify, exalt, revere, sanctify, and crown Your Name, our King. For every mouth will thank You, and

רָקִיעַ, וְעֵינֵינוּ מְאִירוֹת כַּשֶּׁמֶשׁ וְכַיָּרֵחַ, וְיָדֵינוּ פְרוּשׂוֹת כְּנִשְׁרֵי שָׁמָיִם, וְרַגְלֵינוּ קַלּוֹת כָּאַיָּלוֹת, אֵין אֲנַחְנוּ מַסְפִּיקִים לְהוֹדוֹת לְךָ יְיָ אֱלֹהֵינוּ וֵאלֹהֵי אֲבוֹתֵינוּ, וּלְבָרֵךְ אֶת שְׁמֶךָ עַל אַחַת מֵאֶלֶף אַלְפֵי אֲלָפִים וְרִבֵּי רְבָבוֹת פְּעָמִים, הַטּוֹבוֹת שֶׁעָשִׂיתָ עִם אֲבוֹתֵינוּ וְעִמָּנוּ. מִמִּצְרַיִם גְּאַלְתָּנוּ יְיָ אֱלֹהֵינוּ וּמִבֵּית עֲבָדִים פְּדִיתָנוּ, בְּרָעָב זַנְתָּנוּ וּבְשָׂבָע כִּלְכַּלְתָּנוּ, מֵחֶרֶב הִצַּלְתָּנוּ וּמִדֶּבֶר מִלַּטְתָּנוּ, וּמֵחֳלָיִם רָעִים וְנֶאֱמָנִים דִּלִּיתָנוּ. עַד הֵנָּה עֲזָרוּנוּ רַחֲמֶיךָ וְלֹא עֲזָבוּנוּ חֲסָדֶיךָ, וְאַל תִּטְּשֵׁנוּ יְהֹוָה אֱלֹהֵינוּ לָנֶצַח. עַל כֵּן אֵבָרִים שֶׁפִּלַּגְתָּ בָּנוּ, וְרוּחַ וּנְשָׁמָה שֶׁנָּפַחְתָּ בְּאַפֵּינוּ, וְלָשׁוֹן אֲשֶׁר שַׂמְתָּ בְּפִינוּ, הֵן הֵם יוֹדוּ וִיבָרְכוּ וִישַׁבְּחוּ וִיפָאֲרוּ וִירוֹמְמוּ וְיַעֲרִיצוּ

every tongue will swear allegiance to You, and every knee will bend to You, and every person will bow before You. All hearts will fear You and all the innermost feelings will sing to Your Name. As it is written, "All my bones will say, 'Hashem, who is like You?' You save the poor man from one stronger than he, and the poor and needy from one who would rob him" (Tehillim 35:10).

Who is like You, who is equal to You, and who can be compared to You. The Almighty, the Great, the Powerful, the Awesome, most high Almighty, Master of heaven and earth. We will laud You, praise You, and glorify You, and bless Your holy Name, as it is said, "By Dovid: My soul, bless Hashem, and all my innermost being bless His holy Name" (Tehillim 103:1).

The Almighty - in the magnitude of Your strength.
The Great - in the glory of Your Name.
The Powerful - forever.
And the Awesome - through Your awesome deeds.

וְיַקְדִּישׁוּ וְיַמְלִיכוּ אֶת שִׁמְךָ מַלְכֵּנוּ. כִּי כָל פֶּה לְךָ יוֹדֶה, וְכָל לָשׁוֹן לְךָ תִשָּׁבַע, וְכָל בֶּרֶךְ לְךָ תִכְרַע, וְכָל קוֹמָה לְפָנֶיךָ תִשְׁתַּחֲוֶה, וְכָל לְבָבוֹת יִירָאוּךָ, וְכָל קֶרֶב וּכְלָיוֹת יְזַמְּרוּ לִשְׁמֶךָ, כַּדָּבָר שֶׁכָּתוּב, כָּל עַצְמוֹתַי תֹּאמַרְנָה יְהוָה מִי כָמוֹךָ. מַצִּיל עָנִי מֵחָזָק מִמֶּנּוּ, וְעָנִי וְאֶבְיוֹן מִגֹּזְלוֹ.

מִי יִדְמֶה לָּךְ וּמִי יִשְׁוֶה לָּךְ וּמִי יַעֲרָךְ לָךְ, הָאֵל הַגָּדוֹל הַגִּבּוֹר וְהַנּוֹרָא אֵל עֶלְיוֹן, קוֹנֵה שָׁמַיִם וָאָרֶץ. נְהַלֶּלְךָ וּנְשַׁבֵּחֲךָ וּנְפָאֶרְךָ וּנְבָרֵךְ אֶת שֵׁם קָדְשֶׁךָ, כָּאָמוּר, לְדָוִד, בָּרְכִי נַפְשִׁי אֶת יְהוָה, וְכָל קְרָבַי אֶת שֵׁם קָדְשׁוֹ.

הָאֵל בְּתַעֲצֻמוֹת עֻזֶּךָ,
הַגָּדוֹל בִּכְבוֹד שְׁמֶךָ,
הַגִּבּוֹר לָנֶצַח
וְהַנּוֹרָא בְּנוֹרְאוֹתֶיךָ.

The King who sits on a high and exalted throne.

He Who lives forever, exalted and holy is His Name. And it is written, "Rejoice in Hashem, you righteous; for the upright, praise is fitting" (*Tehillim* 33:1).

By the mouth of the upright,
    You shall be praised.
And by the words of the righteous,
    You shall be blessed.
And by the tongue of the pious,
    You shall be exalted.
And amidst the holy,
    You shall be sanctified.

And in the assemblies of myriads of Your people, the house of Yisroel, with joyful song, Your Name, our King, will be glorified in every generation. For it is the duty of all creatures before You, Hashem our God and God of our fathers, to thank, laud, praise, glorify, exalt, honor, bless, extol, and acclaim, even beyond all the words of songs and praises of Dovid, son of Yishai, Your servant, Your annointed.

הַמֶּלֶךְ הַיּוֹשֵׁב עַל כִּסֵּא רָם וְנִשָּׂא.

שׁוֹכֵן עַד מָרוֹם וְקָדוֹשׁ שְׁמוֹ, וְכָתוּב, רַנְּנוּ צַדִּיקִים בַּיהֹוָה, לַיְשָׁרִים נָאוָה תְהִלָּה.

בְּפִי יְשָׁרִים תִּתְהַלָּל,
וּבְדִבְרֵי צַדִּיקִים תִּתְבָּרַךְ,
וּבִלְשׁוֹן חֲסִידִים תִּתְרוֹמָם,
וּבְקֶרֶב קְדוֹשִׁים תִּתְקַדָּשׁ.

וּבְמַקְהֲלוֹת רִבְבוֹת עַמְּךָ בֵּית יִשְׂרָאֵל, בְּרִנָּה יִתְפָּאַר שִׁמְךָ מַלְכֵּנוּ בְּכָל דּוֹר וָדוֹר, שֶׁכֵּן חוֹבַת כָּל הַיְצוּרִים לְפָנֶיךָ יְיָ אֱלֹהֵינוּ וֵאלֹהֵי אֲבוֹתֵינוּ, לְהוֹדוֹת לְהַלֵּל לְשַׁבֵּחַ לְפָאֵר לְרוֹמֵם לְהַדֵּר לְבָרֵךְ לְעַלֵּה וּלְקַלֵּס, עַל כָּל דִּבְרֵי שִׁירוֹת וְתִשְׁבָּחוֹת דָּוִד בֶּן יִשַׁי עַבְדְּךָ מְשִׁיחֶךָ:

Praised be Your Name for ever our King, Almighty, the Great and Holy King, in heaven and on earth. For You it is fitting, Hashem our God and God of our fathers, song and praise,
lauding and tune,
power and dominion,
victory, greatness, and strength,
extolling and splendor,
holiness and sovereignty,
blessings and thanksgivings,
for now and forever. Blessed are You Hashem, King, Who is extolled with praises.

יִשְׁתַּבַּח שִׁמְךָ לָעַד מַלְכֵּנוּ, הָאֵל הַמֶּלֶךְ הַגָּדוֹל וְהַקָּדוֹשׁ בַּשָּׁמַיִם וּבָאָרֶץ, כִּי לְךָ נָאֶה יְיָ אֱלֹהֵינוּ וֵאלֹהֵי אֲבוֹתֵינוּ, שִׁיר וּשְׁבָחָה הַלֵּל וְזִמְרָה עֹז וּמֶמְשָׁלָה נֶצַח גְּדֻלָּה וּגְבוּרָה תְּהִלָּה וְתִפְאֶרֶת קְדֻשָּׁה וּמַלְכוּת בְּרָכוֹת וְהוֹדָאוֹת מֵעַתָּה וְעַד עוֹלָם, בָּרוּךְ אַתָּה יְיָ מֶלֶךְ מְהֻלָּל בַּתִּשְׁבָּחוֹת:

Before drinking the fourth cup, one should think that he is about to fulfill the mitzvah of drinking the last of the four cups.
Effort should be made to drink a reviyis in order to recite the b'racha acharona.
A man should recline when drinking the fourth cup.
If a man forgot to recline, he should not drink another cup.
According to some opinions, one should try to drink the fourth cup before halachic midnight.

The Guidelines Haggadah   132

Blessed are You, Hashem our God, King of the universe, Who creates the fruit of the vine.

בָּרוּךְ אַתָּה יְיָ אֱלֹהֵינוּ מֶלֶךְ הָעוֹלָם, בּוֹרֵא פְּרִי הַגָּפֶן:

379. The *B'racha Acharona*, *Al Hagefen*, is recited by everyone who drank a *reviyis*. When reciting the *b'racha*, one should have in mind that it also applies to the other three cups of wine.

380. If a person was unable to drink a *reviyis* for the fourth cup, but drank a *reviyis* for the third cup, he should recite the *b'racha Al Hagefen*.

381. If he did not drink a *reviyis* for either the third or fourth cup, he should listen to someone else who is reciting the *b'racha* and have in mind to be included.

382. If one forgot to include the words *chag hamatzos* in *Al Hagefen* (or *Retzei* on Shabbos), the *b'racha* should not be repeated.

Blessed are You, Hashem our God, King of the universe, for the vine and the fruit of the vine, and for the produce of the field, and for the desirable, good, and spacious land that You were pleased to give as a heritage to our forefathers, to eat of its fruit and to be satisfied with its goodness. Have compassion, Hashem our God, on Yisroel your people, on Yerushalayim Your city, on Zion the abode of Your glory, on Your altar,

בָּרוּךְ אַתָּה יְיָ אֱלֹהֵינוּ מֶלֶךְ הָעוֹלָם, עַל הַגֶּפֶן וְעַל פְּרִי הַגֶּפֶן וְעַל תְּנוּבַת הַשָּׂדֶה וְעַל אֶרֶץ חֶמְדָּה טוֹבָה וּרְחָבָה, שֶׁרָצִיתָ וְהִנְחַלְתָּ לַאֲבוֹתֵינוּ, לֶאֱכֹל מִפִּרְיָהּ וְלִשְׂבֹּעַ מִטּוּבָהּ. רַחֵם (נָא) יְיָ אֱלֹהֵינוּ עַל יִשְׂרָאֵל עַמֶּךָ, וְעַל יְרוּשָׁלַיִם עִירֶךָ, וְעַל צִיּוֹן מִשְׁכַּן כְּבוֹדֶךָ וְעַל מִזְבַּחֶךָ וְעַל הֵיכָלֶךָ. וּבְנֵה יְרוּשָׁלַיִם עִיר הַקֹּדֶשׁ בִּמְהֵרָה בְיָמֵינוּ,

and on Your sanctuary. And rebuild Yerushalayim the holy city speedily in our days, bring us up into it, and make us happy with its rebuilding. Let us eat from its fruit and be satisfied with its goodness, and bless You upon it in holiness and purity.

וְהַעֲלֵנוּ לְתוֹכָהּ וְשַׂמְּחֵנוּ בְּבִנְיָנָהּ וְנֹאכַל מִפִּרְיָהּ וְנִשְׂבַּע מִטּוּבָהּ, וּנְבָרֶכְךָ עָלֶיהָ בִּקְדֻשָּׁה וּבְטָהֳרָה,

(on Shabbos add: **and may it please You to strengthen us on this day of Shabbos**)

(On Shabbos)
וּרְצֵה וְהַחֲלִיצֵנוּ בְּיוֹם הַשַּׁבָּת הַזֶּה,

And make us happy on this Festival of Matzos, for You Hashem are good, and do good to all, and we thank You for the land and for the fruit of the vine. Blessed are You Hashem, for the land and for the fruit of the vine (its vine).

וְשַׂמְּחֵנוּ בְּיוֹם חַג הַמַּצּוֹת הַזֶּה,

כִּי אַתָּה יְיָ טוֹב וּמֵטִיב לַכֹּל, וְנוֹדֶה לְּךָ עַל הָאָרֶץ וְעַל פְּרִי הַגָּפֶן: בָּרוּךְ אַתָּה יְיָ, עַל הָאָרֶץ וְעַל פְּרִי הַגָּפֶן (גַּפְנָהּ):

Nirtzah

The Seder is accepted

The order of the Pesach Seder is ended according to its laws and rules. Just as we have been privileged to perform it, so may we merit to bring the *Korban Pesach*. O Pure One, Who dwells on high, raise up the congregation that cannot be counted. Soon, lead the offshoots of Your plants joyously, redeemed to Tziyon.

Next year in Yerushalayim!

חֲסַל סִדּוּר פֶּסַח כְּהִלְכָתוֹ, כְּכָל מִשְׁפָּטוֹ וְחֻקָּתוֹ, כַּאֲשֶׁר זָכִינוּ לְסַדֵּר אוֹתוֹ, כֵּן נִזְכֶּה לַעֲשׂוֹתוֹ, זָךְ שׁוֹכֵן מְעוֹנָה, קוֹמֵם קְהַל עֲדַת מִי מָנָה, בְּקָרוֹב נַהֵל נִטְעֵי כַנָּה, פְּדוּיִם לְצִיּוֹן בְּרִנָּה.

לְשָׁנָה הַבָּאָה בִּירוּשָׁלָיִם:

The final part of the Haggadah comprises songs of praise to Hashem. These songs were added later in order to express our desire to praise Hashem with even greater enthusiasm and joy. A person who is completely exhausted is not obligated to say them.

‏וּבְכֵן וַיְהִי בַּחֲצִי הַלַּיְלָה:

And it happened at midnight

Then, You performed many		‏אָז רוֹב נִסִּים הִפְלֵאתָ
wonderous miracles	at night.	‏בַּלַּיְלָה.
At the start of the watch	this night.	‏בְּרֹאשׁ אַשְׁמוֹרֶת זֶה הַלַּיְלָה.
To the righteous Avraham You		‏גֵּר צֶדֶק נִצַּחְתּוֹ כְּנֶחֱלַק לוֹ
gave victory as You divided	the night.	‏לַיְלָה.
And it happened at midnight.		‏וַיְהִי בַּחֲצִי הַלַּיְלָה:

You judged Avimelech in a dream	at night.	‏דַּנְתָּ מֶלֶךְ גְּרָר בַּחֲלוֹם הַלַּיְלָה.
You frightened Lavan in the dark of	night.	‏הִפְחַדְתָּ אֲרַמִּי בְּאֶמֶשׁ לַיְלָה.
Yisroel wrestled with an angel		‏וַיָּשַׂר יִשְׂרָאֵל לְמַלְאָךְ וַיּוּכַל לוֹ
and defeated him	at night.	‏לַיְלָה.
And it happened at midnight.		‏וַיְהִי בַּחֲצִי הַלַּיְלָה:

The firstborn Egyptian sons You crushed at	midnight.	‏זֶרַע בְּכוֹרֵי פַתְרוֹס מָחַצְתָּ בַּחֲצִי הַלַּיְלָה.
They did not find their wealth		‏חֵילָם לֹא מָצְאוּ בְּקוּמָם
when they arose	at night.	‏בַּלַּיְלָה.
The army of Sisera You trampled with the		‏טִיסַת נְגִיד חֲרוֹשֶׁת סִלִּיתָ בְּכוֹכְבֵי
stars of	night.	‏לַיְלָה.
And it happened at midnight.		‏וַיְהִי בַּחֲצִי הַלַּיְלָה:

Sancheriv planned to raise his hand against
   Yerushalayim, but You withered his soldiers'
   corpses   at night.
The idol *Bel* and its pedestal You
   overturned in the dark of   night.
To Daniel, the man of Your delight,
   was revealed the secret of the vision   at night.

          And it happened at midnight.

Belshatzar, who became drunk with
   the *Beis Hamikdash* vessels, was killed   at night.
Daniel, saved from the lions'' den,
   interpreted the terrors of the   night.
Haman nursed hatred and wrote edicts   at night.

          And it happened at midnight.

You aroused Your triumph over him
   by disturbing Achashverosh's sleep   at night.
You will trample the enemies of those who
   ask Hashem, "What will be of the long   night?"
Hashem will shout like a watchman and say,
   "Morning has come (for the righteous),
   and (for the sinners)   night".

          And it happened at midnight.

Bring the day (of *Mashiach*) that is
   neither day nor   night.
Exalted God, show that Yours is the day and the night.
Appoint guards for Your city all day and all   night.
Brighten like the light of day, the darkness of night.

          And it happened at midnight.

יָעַץ מְחָרֵף לְנוֹפֵף אִוּוּי הוֹבַשְׁתָּ פְגָרָיו בַּלַּיְלָה.

כָּרַע בֵּל וּמַצָּבוֹ בְּאִישׁוֹן לַיְלָה.

לְאִישׁ חֲמוּדוֹת נִגְלָה רָז חָזוֹת לַיְלָה.

וַיְהִי בַּחֲצִי הַלַּיְלָה:

מִשְׁתַּכֵּר בִּכְלֵי קֹדֶשׁ נֶהֱרַג בּוֹ בַּלַּיְלָה.

נוֹשַׁע מִבּוֹר אֲרָיוֹת פּוֹתֵר בְּעִתוּתֵי לַיְלָה.

שִׂנְאָה נָטַר אֲגָגִי וְכָתַב סְפָרִים בַּלַּיְלָה.

וַיְהִי בַּחֲצִי הַלַּיְלָה:

עוֹרַרְתָּ נִצְחֲךָ עָלָיו בְּנֶדֶד שְׁנַת לַיְלָה.

פּוּרָה תִדְרוֹךְ לְשׁוֹמֵר מַה מִּלַּיְלָה.

צָרַח כַּשּׁוֹמֵר וְשָׂח אָתָא בֹקֶר וְגַם לַיְלָה.

וַיְהִי בַּחֲצִי הַלַּיְלָה:

קָרֵב יוֹם אֲשֶׁר הוּא לֹא יוֹם וְלֹא לַיְלָה.

רָם הוֹדַע כִּי לְךָ הַיּוֹם אַף לְךָ הַלַּיְלָה.

שׁוֹמְרִים הַפְקֵד לְעִירְךָ כָּל הַיּוֹם וְכָל הַלַּיְלָה.

תָּאִיר כְּאוֹר יוֹם חֶשְׁכַּת לַיְלָה.

וַיְהִי בַּחֲצִי הַלַּיְלָה:

> **In Eretz Yisroel the following is said on the first night.**
> **In Chutz La'aretz the following is said on the second night.**

וּבְכֵן וַאֲמַרְתֶּם זֶבַח פֶּסַח:

And you shall say, "This is the *Korban Pesach*"

Your great powers You wonderously displayed on Pesach.	בַּפֶּסַח.	אֹמֶץ גְּבוּרוֹתֶיךָ הִפְלֵאתָ
Above all festivals You elevated Pesach.	פֶּסַח.	בְּרֹאשׁ כָּל מוֹעֲדוֹת נִשֵּׂאתָ
To Avraham You revealed the midnight Exodus of Pesach.	פֶּסַח.	גִּלִּיתָ לְאֶזְרָחִי חֲצוֹת לֵיל
And you shall say, "This is the *Korban Pesach*".		וַאֲמַרְתֶּם זֶבַח פֶּסַח:

At his door You knocked in the heat of the day on Pesach.	בַּפֶּסַח.	דְּלָתָיו דָּפַקְתָּ כְּחֹם הַיּוֹם
He served the sparkling angels matza cakes on Pesach.	בַּפֶּסַח.	הִסְעִיד נוֹצְצִים עֻגוֹת מַצּוֹת
And he ran to the cattle, symbolic of the *Korban Chagiga* of Pesach.	פֶּסַח.	וְאֶל הַבָּקָר רָץ זֵכֶר לְשׁוֹר עֵרֶךְ
And you shall say, "This is the *Korban Pesach*".		וַאֲמַרְתֶּם זֶבַח פֶּסַח:

The men of Sedom angered Hashem and were consumed by fire on Pesach.	בַּפֶּסַח.	זוֹעֲמוּ סְדוֹמִים וְלֹהֲטוּ בָּאֵשׁ
Lot was rescued from their midst and baked matzos at the demise (of Sedom) on Pesach.	פֶּסַח.	חֻלַּץ לוֹט מֵהֶם וּמַצּוֹת אָפָה בְּקֵץ
You swept clean the Egyptian cities of Mof and Nof when You passed through on Pesach.	בַּפֶּסַח.	טֵאטֵאתָ אַדְמַת מוֹף וְנוֹף בְּעָבְרְךָ
And you shall say, "This is the *Korban Pesach*".		וַאֲמַרְתֶּם זֶבַח פֶּסַח:

The Guidelines Haggadah

Hashem, You crushed every firstborn
    of Egypt on the watchnight   of Pesach.
Mighty One, You skipped over Your firstborn
    in the merit of the blood of (the *Korban*)   *Pesach*.
So as not to let the destroyer enter
my doors   on Pesach.
    And you shall say, "This is the *Korban Pesach*".

The locked city of Yericho was
    beseiged at the time of   Pesach.
Midyan was destroyed in the merit
of the *omer* of barley   on Pesach.
    The mighty nobles of Pul and Lud (Assyria)
were burned in a great blaze   on Pesach.
    And you shall say, "This is the *Korban Pesach*".

Sancheriv would have remained
    standing at the city Nov if not for   Pesach.
A hand wrote on the wall about
    Bavel"s destruction   on Pesach.
They arranged the watchman while
    they prepared the festive table on   Pesach.
And you shall say, "This is the *Korban Pesach*".

Esther gathered the people for a
    three day fast   on Pesach.
Haman, the head of Amalek, You
    hanged on a fifty *amah* gallows   on Pesach.
Double misfortune You will bring
    in an instant upon Edom   on Pesach.
May Your hand be strong and Your
    right arm exalted as on that night
    when You sanctified the festival   of Pesach.
And you shall say, "This is the *Korban Pesach*".

יָהּ רֹאשׁ כָּל אוֹן מָחַצְתָּ בְּלֵיל שִׁמּוּר פֶּסַח.

כַּבִּיר עַל בֵּן בְּכוֹר פָּסַחְתָּ בְּדַם פֶּסַח.

לְבִלְתִּי תֵּת מַשְׁחִית לָבֹא בִּפְתָחַי בַּפֶּסַח.

וַאֲמַרְתֶּם זֶבַח פֶּסַח:

מִסְגֶּרֶת סֻגְּרָה בְּעִתּוֹתֵי פֶּסַח.

נִשְׁמְדָה מִדְיָן בִּצְלִיל שְׂעוֹרֵי עוֹמֶר פֶּסַח.

שׂוֹרְפוּ מִשְׁמַנֵּי פּוּל וְלוּד בִּיקַד יְקוֹד פֶּסַח.

וַאֲמַרְתֶּם זֶבַח פֶּסַח:

עוֹד הַיּוֹם בְּנֹב לַעֲמוֹד עַד גָּעָה עוֹנַת פֶּסַח.

פַּס יָד כָּתְבָה לְקַעֲקֵעַ צוּל בַּפֶּסַח.

צָפֹה הַצָּפִית עָרוֹךְ הַשֻּׁלְחָן בַּפֶּסַח.

וַאֲמַרְתֶּם זֶבַח פֶּסַח:

קָהָל כִּנְּסָה הֲדַסָּה צוֹם לְשַׁלֵּשׁ בַּפֶּסַח.

רֹאשׁ מִבֵּית רָשָׁע מָחַצְתָּ בְּעֵץ חֲמִשִּׁים בַּפֶּסַח.

שְׁתֵּי אֵלֶּה רֶגַע תָּבִיא לְעוּצִית בַּפֶּסַח.

תָּעֹז יָדְךָ וְתָרוּם יְמִינְךָ כְּלֵיל הִתְקַדֵּשׁ חַג פֶּסַח.

וַאֲמַרְתֶּם זֶבַח פֶּסַח:

כִּי לוֹ נָאֶה, כִּי לוֹ יָאֶה.

To Him it is becoming, to Him it is fitting.

Mighty in Kingship, truly chosen, His companies
of angels say to Him:
To You (are the heavens) and to You (is the earth).
To You, because it is appropriate to You!
To You (is the day), to You (is the night)!
To You Hashem is Kingship!
To Him it is becoming, to Him it is fitting.

אַדִּיר בִּמְלוּכָה, בָּחוּר כַּהֲלָכָה, גְּדוּדָיו יֹאמְרוּ
לוֹ.
לְךָ וּלְךָ, לְךָ כִּי לְךָ, לְךָ אַף לְךָ, לְךָ יְיָ הַמַּמְלָכָה,
כִּי לוֹ נָאֶה, כִּי לוֹ יָאֶה.

Surrounded (by angels) in Kingship, truly glorious,
His pious ones say to Him:
To You (are the heavens) and to You (is the earth).
To You, because it is appropriate to You!
To You (is the day), to You (is the night)!
To You Hashem is Kingship!
To Him it is becoming, to Him it is fitting.

דָּגוּל בִּמְלוּכָה, הָדוּר כַּהֲלָכָה, וָתִיקָיו יֹאמְרוּ
לוֹ.
לְךָ וּלְךָ, לְךָ כִּי לְךָ, לְךָ אַף לְךָ, לְךָ יְיָ הַמַּמְלָכָה,
כִּי לוֹ נָאֶה, כִּי לוֹ יָאֶה.

Pure in Kingship, truly powerful, His princely angels
say to Him:
To You (are the heavens) and to You (is the earth).
To You, because it is appropriate to You!
To You (is the day), to You (is the night)!
To You Hashem is Kingship!
To Him it is becoming, to Him it is fitting.

זַכַּאי בִּמְלוּכָה, חָסִין כַּהֲלָכָה, טַפְסְרָיו יֹאמְרוּ
לוֹ.
לְךָ וּלְךָ, לְךָ כִּי לְךָ, לְךָ אַף לְךָ, לְךָ יְיָ הַמַּמְלָכָה,
כִּי לוֹ נָאֶה, כִּי לוֹ יָאֶה.

Alone in Kingship, truly mighty, His scholars say to
Him:

יָחִיד בִּמְלוּכָה, כַּבִּיר כַּהֲלָכָה, לִמּוּדָיו יֹאמְרוּ לוֹ.

The Guidelines Haggadah

To You (are the heavens) and to You (is the earth).
To You, because it is appropriate to You!
To You (is the day), to You (is the night)!
To You Hashem is Kingship!
To Him it is becoming, to Him it is fitting.

Ruler in Kingship, truly awesome, His surrounding angels say to Him:
To You (are the heavens) and to You (is the earth). To You, because it is appropriate to You! To You (is the day), to You (is the night)! To You Hashem is Kingship! To Him it is becoming, to Him it is fitting.

Humble in Kingship, truly a redeemer, His righteous say to Him:
To You (are the heavens) and to You (is the earth). To You, because it is appropriate to You! To You (is the day), to You (is the night)! To You Hashem is Kingship! To Him it is becoming, to Him it is fitting.

Holy in Kingship, truly merciful, His hosts of angels say to Him:
To You (are the heavens) and to You (is the earth).
To You, because it is appropriate to You!
To You (is the day), to You (is the night)!
To You Hashem is Kingship!
To Him it is becoming, to Him it is fitting.

Powerful in Kingship, truly sustaining, His perfect ones say to Him:
To You (are the heavens) and to You (is the earth).
To You, because it is appropriate to You!
To You (is the day), to You (is the night)!
To You Hashem is kingship!
To Him it is becoming, to Him it is fitting.

לְךָ וּלְךָ, לְךָ כִּי לְךָ, לְךָ אַף לְךָ, לְךָ יְיָ הַמַּמְלָכָה, כִּי לוֹ נָאֶה, כִּי לוֹ יָאֶה.

מוֹשֵׁל בִּמְלוּכָה, נוֹרָא כַּהֲלָכָה, סְבִיבָיו יֹאמְרוּ לוֹ.
לְךָ וּלְךָ, לְךָ כִּי לְךָ, לְךָ אַף לְךָ, לְךָ יְיָ הַמַּמְלָכָה, כִּי לוֹ נָאֶה, כִּי לוֹ יָאֶה.

עָנָיו בִּמְלוּכָה, פּוֹדֶה כַּהֲלָכָה, צַדִּיקָיו יֹאמְרוּ לוֹ.
לְךָ וּלְךָ, לְךָ כִּי לְךָ, לְךָ אַף לְךָ, לְךָ יְיָ הַמַּמְלָכָה, כִּי לוֹ נָאֶה, כִּי לוֹ יָאֶה.

קָדוֹשׁ בִּמְלוּכָה, רַחוּם כַּהֲלָכָה, שִׁנְאַנָּיו יֹאמְרוּ לוֹ.
לְךָ וּלְךָ, לְךָ כִּי לְךָ, לְךָ אַף לְךָ, לְךָ יְיָ הַמַּמְלָכָה, כִּי לוֹ נָאֶה, כִּי לוֹ יָאֶה.

תַּקִּיף בִּמְלוּכָה, תּוֹמֵךְ כַּהֲלָכָה, תְּמִימָיו יֹאמְרוּ לוֹ.
לְךָ וּלְךָ, לְךָ כִּי לְךָ, לְךָ אַף לְךָ, לְךָ יְיָ הַמַּמְלָכָה, כִּי לוֹ נָאֶה, כִּי לוֹ יָאֶה.

אַדִּיר הוּא
He is glorious

He is glorious.
May He soon build His house, speedily, speedily in our days, soon! Build O God! Build O God! Build Your house soon!

He is chosen, He is great, He is surrounded (by angels).
May He soon build His house, speedily, speedily in our days, soon! Build O God! Build O God! Build Your house soon!

He is splendid, He is faithful, He is immaculate, He is pious.
May He soon build His house, speedily, speedily in our days, soon! Build O God! Build O God! Build Your house soon!

אַדִּיר הוּא יִבְנֶה בֵיתוֹ בְּקָרוֹב, בִּמְהֵרָה בִּמְהֵרָה בְּיָמֵינוּ בְּקָרוֹב, אֵל בְּנֵה אֵל בְּנֵה, בְּנֵה בֵיתְךָ בְּקָרוֹב.

בָּחוּר הוּא, גָּדוֹל הוּא, דָּגוּל הוּא, יִבְנֶה בֵיתוֹ בְּקָרוֹב. בִּמְהֵרָה בִּמְהֵרָה בְּיָמֵינוּ בְּקָרוֹב, אֵל בְּנֵה אֵל בְּנֵה, בְּנֵה בֵיתְךָ בְּקָרוֹב.

הָדוּר הוּא, וָתִיק הוּא, זַכַּאי הוּא, חָסִיד הוּא, יִבְנֶה בֵיתוֹ בְּקָרוֹב, בִּמְהֵרָה בְּיָמֵינוּ בְּקָרוֹב, אֵל בְּנֵה אֵל בְּנֵה, בְּנֵה בֵיתְךָ בְּקָרוֹב.

He is pure, He is alone, He is mighty, He is consistent, He is majestic, He is awesome, He is sublime, He is powerful, He is redeeming, He is righteous.

May He soon build His house, speedily, speedily in our days, soon! Build O God! Build O God! Build Your house soon!

He is holy, He is compassionate, He is unlimited, He is omnipotent.

May He soon build His house, speedily, speedily in our days, soon! Build O God! Build O God! Build Your house soon!

טָהוֹר הוּא, יָחִיד הוּא, כַּבִּיר הוּא, לָמוּד הוּא, מֶלֶךְ הוּא, נוֹרָא הוּא, סַגִּיב הוּא, עִזּוּז הוּא, פּוֹדֶה הוּא, צַדִּיק הוּא, יִבְנֶה בֵיתוֹ בְּקָרוֹב, בִּמְהֵרָה בִּמְהֵרָה בְּיָמֵינוּ בְּקָרוֹב, אֵל בְּנֵה אֵל בְּנֵה, בְּנֵה בֵיתְךָ בְּקָרוֹב.

קָדוֹשׁ הוּא, רַחוּם הוּא, שַׁדַּי הוּא, תַּקִּיף הוּא, יִבְנֶה בֵיתוֹ בְּקָרוֹב, בִּמְהֵרָה בִּמְהֵרָה בְּיָמֵינוּ בְּקָרוֹב, אֵל בְּנֵה אֵל בְּנֵה, בְּנֵה בֵיתְךָ בְּקָרוֹב.

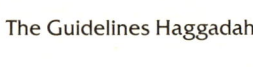

אֶחָד מִי יוֹדֵעַ

Who knows One?

Who knows One? I know One!
One is our God, Who is in the Heaven and on Earth.

אֶחָד מִי יוֹדֵעַ, אֶחָד אֲנִי יוֹדֵעַ, אֶחָד אֱלֹהֵינוּ שֶׁבַּשָּׁמַיִם וּבָאָרֶץ.

Who knows Two? I know Two!
Two are the tablets of the covenant; One is our God, Who is in the Heaven and on Earth.

שְׁנַיִם מִי יוֹדֵעַ, שְׁנַיִם אֲנִי יוֹדֵעַ. שְׁנֵי לוּחוֹת הַבְּרִית, אֶחָד אֱלֹהֵינוּ שֶׁבַּשָּׁמַיִם וּבָאָרֶץ.

Who knows Three? I know Three!
Three are the Patriarchs; Two are the tablets of the covenant; One is our God, Who is in the Heaven and on Earth.

שְׁלֹשָׁה מִי יוֹדֵעַ, שְׁלֹשָׁה אֲנִי יוֹדֵעַ, שְׁלֹשָׁה אָבוֹת, שְׁנֵי לוּחוֹת הַבְּרִית, אֶחָד אֱלֹהֵינוּ שֶׁבַּשָּׁמַיִם וּבָאָרֶץ.

Who knows Four? I know Four!
Four are the Matriarchs; Three are the Patriarchs; Two are the tablets of the covenant; One is our God, Who is in the Heaven and on Earth.

אַרְבַּע מִי יוֹדֵעַ, אַרְבַּע אֲנִי יוֹדֵעַ, אַרְבַּע אִמָּהוֹת, שְׁלֹשָׁה אָבוֹת, שְׁנֵי לוּחוֹת הַבְּרִית, אֶחָד אֱלֹהֵינוּ שֶׁבַּשָּׁמַיִם וּבָאָרֶץ.

Who knows Five? I know Five!
Five are the books of the Torah; Four are the Matriarchs; Three are the Patriarchs; Two are the tablets of the covenant; One is our God, Who is in the Heaven and on Earth.

Who knows Six? I know Six!
Six are the orders of the Mishna, Five are the books of the Torah; Four are the Matriarchs; Three are the Patriarchs; Two are the tablets of the covenant; One is our God, Who is in the Heaven and on Earth.

Who knows Seven? I know Seven!
Seven are the days of the week; Six are the orders of the Mishna; Five are the books of the Torah; Four are the Matriarchs; Three are the Patriarchs; Two are the tablets of the covenant; One is our God, Who is in the Heaven and on Earth.

Who knows Eight? I know Eight!
Eight are the days of circumcision; Seven are the days of the week; Six are the orders of the Mishna; Five are the books of the Torah; Four

חֲמִשָׁה מִי יוֹדֵעַ, חֲמִשָׁה אֲנִי יוֹדֵעַ, חֲמִשָׁה חוּמְשֵׁי תוֹרָה, אַרְבַּע אִמָּהוֹת, שְׁלֹשָׁה אָבוֹת, שְׁנֵי לוּחוֹת הַבְּרִית, אֶחָד אֱלֹהֵינוּ שֶׁבַּשָּׁמַיִם וּבָאָרֶץ.

שִׁשָּׁה מִי יוֹדֵעַ, שִׁשָּׁה אֲנִי יוֹדֵעַ, שִׁשָּׁה סִדְרֵי מִשְׁנָה, חֲמִשָׁה חוּמְשֵׁי תוֹרָה, אַרְבַּע אִמָּהוֹת, שְׁלֹשָׁה אָבוֹת, שְׁנֵי לוּחוֹת הַבְּרִית, אֶחָד אֱלֹהֵינוּ שֶׁבַּשָּׁמַיִם וּבָאָרֶץ.

שִׁבְעָה מִי יוֹדֵעַ, שִׁבְעָה אֲנִי יוֹדֵעַ, שִׁבְעָה יְמֵי שַׁבַּתָּא, שִׁשָּׁה סִדְרֵי מִשְׁנָה, חֲמִשָׁה חוּמְשֵׁי תוֹרָה, אַרְבַּע אִמָּהוֹת, שְׁלֹשָׁה אָבוֹת, שְׁנֵי לוּחוֹת הַבְּרִית, אֶחָד אֱלֹהֵינוּ שֶׁבַּשָּׁמַיִם וּבָאָרֶץ.

שְׁמוֹנָה מִי יוֹדֵעַ, שְׁמוֹנָה אֲנִי יוֹדֵעַ, שְׁמוֹנָה יְמֵי מִילָה, שִׁבְעָה יְמֵי שַׁבַּתָּא, שִׁשָּׁה סִדְרֵי מִשְׁנָה, חֲמִשָׁה חוּמְשֵׁי תוֹרָה, אַרְבַּע אִמָּהוֹת,

are the Matriarchs; Three are the Patriarchs;
Two are the tablets of the covenant; One is our
God, Who is in the Heaven and on Earth.

Who knows Nine? I know Nine!
Nine are the months of pregnancy; Eight are the
days of circumcision; Seven are the days of the
week; Six are the orders of the Mishna; Five are
the books of the Torah; Four are the Matriarchs;
Three are the Patriarchs; Two are the tablets of
the covenant; One is our God, Who is in the
Heaven and on Earth.

Who knows Ten? I know Ten!
Ten are the Commandments; Nine are the
months of pregnancy; Eight are the days of
circumcision; Seven are the days of the week;
Six are the orders of the Mishna; Five are the
books of the Torah; Four are the Matriarchs;
Three are the Patriarchs; Two are the tablets of
the covenant; One is our God, Who is in the
Heaven and on Earth.

Who knows Eleven? I know Eleven!
Eleven are the stars (in Yosef''s dream); Ten are
the Commandments; Nine are the months of
pregnancy; Eight are the days of circumcision;
Seven are the days of the week; Six are the

שְׁלשָׁה אָבוֹת, שְׁנֵי לוּחוֹת הַבְּרִית, אֶחָד
אֱלֹהֵינוּ שֶׁבַּשָּׁמַיִם וּבָאָרֶץ.

תִּשְׁעָה מִי יוֹדֵעַ, תִּשְׁעָה אֲנִי יוֹדֵעַ, תִּשְׁעָה
יַרְחֵי לֵידָה, שְׁמוֹנָה יְמֵי מִילָה, שִׁבְעָה יְמֵי
שַׁבַּתָּא, שִׁשָּׁה סִדְרֵי מִשְׁנָה, חֲמִשָּׁה חוּמְשֵׁי
תוֹרָה, אַרְבַּע אִמָּהוֹת, שְׁלשָׁה אָבוֹת, שְׁנֵי
לוּחוֹת הַבְּרִית, אֶחָד אֱלֹהֵינוּ שֶׁבַּשָּׁמַיִם וּבָאָרֶץ.

עֲשָׂרָה מִי יוֹדֵעַ, עֲשָׂרָה אֲנִי יוֹדֵעַ, עֲשָׂרָה
דִּבְּרַיָּא, תִּשְׁעָה יַרְחֵי לֵידָה, שְׁמוֹנָה יְמֵי מִילָה,
שִׁבְעָה יְמֵי שַׁבַּתָּא, שִׁשָּׁה סִדְרֵי מִשְׁנָה, חֲמִשָּׁה
חוּמְשֵׁי תוֹרָה, אַרְבַּע אִמָּהוֹת, שְׁלשָׁה אָבוֹת,
שְׁנֵי לוּחוֹת הַבְּרִית, אֶחָד אֱלֹהֵינוּ שֶׁבַּשָּׁמַיִם
וּבָאָרֶץ.

אַחַד עָשָׂר מִי יוֹדֵעַ, אַחַד עָשָׂר אֲנִי יוֹדֵעַ,
אַחַד עָשָׂר כּוֹכְבַיָּא, עֲשָׂרָה דִּבְּרַיָּא, תִּשְׁעָה
יַרְחֵי לֵידָה, שְׁמוֹנָה יְמֵי מִילָה, שִׁבְעָה יְמֵי

orders of the Mishna; Five are the books of the Torah; Four are the Matriarchs; Three are the Patriarchs; Two are the tablets of the covenant; One is our God, Who is in the Heaven and on Earth.

Who knows Twelve? I know Twelve!

Twelve are the tribes; Eleven are the stars; Ten are the Commandments; Nine are the months of pregnancy; Eight are the days of circumcision; Seven are the days of the week; Six are the orders of the Mishna; Five are the books of the Torah; Four are the Matriarchs; Three are the Patriarchs; Two are the tablets of the covenant; One is our God, Who is in the Heaven and on Earth.

Who knows Thirteen? I know Thirteen!

Thirteen are Hashem''s Attributes of Mercy; Twelve are the tribes; Eleven are the stars; Ten are the Commandments; Nine are the months of pregnancy; Eight are the days of circumcision; Seven are the days of the week; Six are the orders of the Mishna; Five are the books of the Torah; Four are the Matriarchs; Three are the Patriarchs; Two are the tablets of the covenant; One is our God, Who is in the Heaven and on Earth.

שַׁבַּתָּא, שִׁשָּׁה סִדְרֵי מִשְׁנָה, חֲמִשָּׁה חוּמְשֵׁי תוֹרָה, אַרְבַּע אִמָּהוֹת, שְׁלֹשָׁה אָבוֹת, שְׁנֵי לוּחוֹת הַבְּרִית, אֶחָד אֱלֹהֵינוּ שֶׁבַּשָּׁמַיִם וּבָאָרֶץ.

שְׁנֵים עָשָׂר מִי יוֹדֵעַ, שְׁנֵים עָשָׂר אֲנִי יוֹדֵעַ, שְׁנֵים עָשָׂר שִׁבְטַיָּא, אַחַד עָשָׂר כּוֹכְבַיָּא, עֲשָׂרָה דִבְּרַיָּא, תִּשְׁעָה יַרְחֵי לֵידָה, שְׁמוֹנָה יְמֵי מִילָה, שִׁבְעָה יְמֵי שַׁבַּתָּא, שִׁשָּׁה סִדְרֵי מִשְׁנָה, חֲמִשָּׁה חוּמְשֵׁי תוֹרָה, אַרְבַּע אִמָּהוֹת, שְׁלֹשָׁה אָבוֹת, שְׁנֵי לוּחוֹת הַבְּרִית, אֶחָד אֱלֹהֵינוּ שֶׁבַּשָּׁמַיִם וּבָאָרֶץ.

שְׁלֹשָׁה עָשָׂר מִי יוֹדֵעַ, שְׁלֹשָׁה עָשָׂר אֲנִי יוֹדֵעַ, שְׁלֹשָׁה עָשָׂר מִדַּיָּא, שְׁנֵים עָשָׂר שִׁבְטַיָּא, אַחַד עָשָׂר כּוֹכְבַיָּא, עֲשָׂרָה דִבְּרַיָּא, תִּשְׁעָה יַרְחֵי לֵידָה, שְׁמוֹנָה יְמֵי מִילָה, שִׁבְעָה יְמֵי שַׁבַּתָּא, שִׁשָּׁה סִדְרֵי מִשְׁנָה, חֲמִשָּׁה חוּמְשֵׁי תוֹרָה, אַרְבַּע אִמָּהוֹת, שְׁלֹשָׁה אָבוֹת, שְׁנֵי לוּחוֹת הַבְּרִית, אֶחָד אֱלֹהֵינוּ שֶׁבַּשָּׁמַיִם וּבָאָרֶץ.

חַד גַּדְיָא, חַד גַּדְיָא

One kid, one kid

The song Chad Gadya should not be understood literally. It is explained by some of the greatest commentaries as an allegorical story imbued with hidden meanings and deep secrets. The Vilna Gaon interprets the song to be a detailed account of the history of the Jewish people from the days of Yaakov Avinu until the time of Mashiach.

One kid, one kid.
That my father bought for two zuzim.
One kid, one kid.

חַד גַּדְיָא, חַד גַּדְיָא.
דְּזַבִּין אַבָּא בִּתְרֵי זוּזֵי. חַד גַּדְיָא, חַד גַּדְיָא.

Then a cat came and ate the kid, that my father bought for two zuzim. One kid, one kid.

וְאָתָא שׁוּנְרָא, וְאָכְלָה לְגַדְיָא, דְּזַבִּין אַבָּא בִּתְרֵי זוּזֵי. חַד גַּדְיָא, חַד גַּדְיָא.

Then a dog came and bit the cat, that ate the kid, that my father bought for two zuzim. One kid, one kid.

וְאָתָא כַלְבָּא, וְנָשַׁךְ לְשׁוּנְרָא, דְּאָכְלָה לְגַדְיָא, דְּזַבִּין אַבָּא בִּתְרֵי זוּזֵי. חַד גַּדְיָא, חַד גַּדְיָא.

The Guidelines Haggadah

Then a stick came and hit the dog, that bit the cat, that ate the kid, that my father bought for two zuzim. One kid, one kid.

וְאָתָא חוּטְרָא, וְהִכָּה לְכַלְבָּא, דְּנָשַׁךְ לְשׁוּנְרָא, דְּאָכְלָה לְגַדְיָא, דְּזַבִּין אַבָּא בִּתְרֵי זוּזֵי. חַד גַּדְיָא, חַד גַּדְיָא.

Then fire came and burned the stick, that hit the dog, that bit the cat, that ate the kid, that my father bought for two zuzim. One kid, one kid.

וְאָתָא נוּרָא, וְשָׂרַף לְחוּטְרָא, דְּהִכָּה לְכַלְבָּא, דְּנָשַׁךְ לְשׁוּנְרָא, דְּאָכְלָה לְגַדְיָא, דְּזַבִּין אַבָּא בִּתְרֵי זוּזֵי. חַד גַּדְיָא, חַד גַּדְיָא.

Then water came and put out the fire, that burned the stick, that hit the dog, that bit the cat, that ate the kid, that my father bought for two zuzim. One kid, one kid.

וְאָתָא מַיָּא, וְכָבָה לְנוּרָא, דְּשָׂרַף לְחוּטְרָא, דְּהִכָּה לְכַלְבָּא, דְּנָשַׁךְ לְשׁוּנְרָא, דְּאָכְלָה לְגַדְיָא, דְּזַבִּין אַבָּא בִּתְרֵי זוּזֵי. חַד גַּדְיָא, חַד גַּדְיָא.

Then an ox came and drank the water, that put out the fire, that burned the stick, that hit the dog, that bit the cat, that ate the kid, that my father bought for two zuzim. One kid, one kid.

וְאָתָא תוֹרָא, וְשָׁתָה לְמַיָּא, דְּכָבָה לְנוּרָא, דְּשָׂרַף לְחוּטְרָא, דְּהִכָּה לְכַלְבָּא, דְּנָשַׁךְ לְשׁוּנְרָא, דְּאָכְלָה לְגַדְיָא, דְּזַבִּין אַבָּא בִּתְרֵי זוּזֵי. חַד גַּדְיָא, חַד גַּדְיָא.

Then the slaughterer came and slaughtered the ox, that drank the water, that put out the fire, that burned the stick, that hit the dog, that bit the cat, that ate the kid, that my father bought for two zuzim. One kid, one kid.

וְאָתָא הַשּׁוֹחֵט, וְשָׁחַט לְתוֹרָא, דְּשָׁתָה לְמַיָּא, דְּכָבָה לְנוּרָא, דְּשָׂרַף לְחוּטְרָא, דְּהִכָּה לְכַלְבָּא, דְּנָשַׁךְ לְשׁוּנְרָא, דְּאָכְלָה לְגַדְיָא, דְּזַבִּין אַבָּא בִּתְרֵי זוּזֵי. חַד גַּדְיָא, חַד גַּדְיָא.

Then The Angel of Death came and killed the slaughterer, who slaughtered the ox, that drank the water, that put out the fire, that burned the stick, that hit the dog, that bit the cat, that ate the kid, that my father bought for two zuzim. One kid, one kid.

וְאָתָא מַלְאַךְ הַמָּוֶת, וְשָׁחַט לְשׁוֹחֵט, דְּשָׁחַט לְתוֹרָא, דְּשָׁתָה לְמַיָּא, דְּכָבָה לְנוּרָא, דְּשָׂרַף לְחוּטְרָא, דְּהִכָּה לְכַלְבָּא, דְּנָשַׁךְ לְשׁוּנְרָא, דְּאָכְלָה לְגַדְיָא, דְּזַבִּין אַבָּא בִּתְרֵי זוּזֵי. חַד גַּדְיָא, חַד גַּדְיָא.

Then The Holy One, Blessed is He, came, and slaughtered the Angel of Death, who killed the slaughterer, who slaughtered the ox, that drank the water, that put out the fire, that burned the stick, that hit the dog, that bit the cat, that ate the kid, that my father bought for two zuzim.

וְאָתָא הַקָּדוֹשׁ בָּרוּךְ הוּא, וְשָׁחַט לְמַלְאַךְ הַמָּוֶת, דְּשָׁחַט לְשׁוֹחֵט, דְּשָׁחַט לְתוֹרָא, דְּשָׁתָה לְמַיָּא, דְּכָבָה לְנוּרָא, דְּשָׂרַף לְחוּטְרָא, דְּהִכָּה לְכַלְבָּא, דְּנָשַׁךְ לְשׁוּנְרָא, דְּאָכְלָה לְגַדְיָא, דְּזַבִּין אַבָּא בִּתְרֵי זוּזֵי.

One kid, one kid.

חַד גַּדְיָא, חַד גַּדְיָא.

383. Some recite *Shir Hashirim* after the Seder.

384. According to the Midrash, *Shir Hashirim* is an allegorical song describing the mutual devotion between Hashem and the Jewish people. Many of the verses refer to the miracles of *Yetzias Mitzrayim*.

385. There is a mitzvah to remain awake as long as possible to study the laws of Pesach and to continue relating the miracles of *Yetzias Mitzrayim*. If a person is overcome by sleep, he is exempt. Similarly, if he will not be able to *daven Shacharis* properly without a good night's sleep, he may retire to bed.

386. Before going to sleep, the custom is to recite only the first paragraph of Shema and the *b'racha Hamapil*. The reason is because the remaining verses are usually said as a protection from danger. On the Seder night, this is unnecessary, since it is a night of Divine protection.

Second Seder in Chutz La'aretz

387. The Seder table must not be arranged until nightfall. If it is *motzai Shabbos*, the women should say *baruch hamavdil bein kodesh lekodesh* before beginning any work.

388. When reciting the Haggadah and when eating the matza, one should have in mind to fulfill a Rabbinic mitzvah.

389. For the first *kezayis* of matza it is sufficient to eat 15 grams. A sick or elderly person may be lenient to eat 10 grams, if necessary. The leader of the Seder should eat 15 grams from the top matza and 15 grams from the middle matza.

390. Some have the custom not to hurry to eat the *Afikoman* before *halachic* midnight.

391. One may have any non-intoxicating drinks after the *Afikoman*.

392. One may retire to bed immediately after the Seder.

Glossary

Al Hagefen - B'racha recited after drinking wine or grape juice.

Al Netilas Yadayim - B'racha recited after washing hands.

Arizal - Rabbi Yitzchak Luria (1534-1572), considered to be one of the greatest kabbalists.

Bamidbar - The book of Numbers.

Bedikas Chametz - The search for chametz.

Beis Hamikdash - The Holy Temple.

Bensch - To recite grace after meals.

Benschers - Book from which *bensching* is recited.

Bereishis - The book of Genesis.

Borei P'ri Ha''adama - B'racha recited for vegetables (lit. Who creates the fruit of the ground).

Borei Pri Ha''eitz - B'racha recited for fruit (lit. Who creates the fruit of the tree).

Borei P'ri Hagafen - B'racha recited for wine and grape juice (lit. Who creates the fruit of the vine).

B'racha (pl. *brachos*) - A blessing.

B'racha Acharona - B'racha recited after eating or drinking.

Bris - Circumcision.

Bris Bein Habesarim - The covenant between the parts.

Challah - Tithe taken from dough.

Chas veshalom - God forbid.

Chazal - The Sages.

Chol Hamoed - The intermediate days of the festival.

Chametz - Leaven, which may not be owned or eaten during Pesach.

Chutz La'aretz - The Diaspora.

Daven - To pray.

Devarim - The book of Deuteronomy.

Divrei Hayamim - The book of Chronicles.

Eiruv - Enclosure of a public domain which transfers it into a private one in order to permit objects to be carried on Shabbos.

Eiruv Tavshilin - Foods prepared before Yom Tov to allow preparations to be made on Friday for Shabbos. This is required when Yom Tov is on the day(s) immediately preceding Shabbos.

Eliyahu Hanavi - Elijah the prophet.

Eretz Yisroel - The land of Israel.

Erev Pesach - The day before Pesach.

Erev Shabbos - The day before Shabbos.

Erev Yom Tov - The day before a festival.

Gebroktz - Soaked matzo or matzo meal.

Halacha (pl. *halachos*) - Jewish law.

Halachic dawn - 72 *halachic* minutes before sunrise.

Halachic hour - 1/12 day, reckoned from sunrise to sunset (or dawn to nightfall).

Halachic midday - The midpoint between sunrise and sunset.

Hallel - Psalms of praise recited on festive days.

Hamavdil - The fourth *b'racha* of *Havdalah*.

Hamotzi - The blessing recited for bread (lit. Who takes bread out of the ground').

Hashem - God.

Hatov Vehameitiv - B'racha recited for a superior wine in certain circumstances.

Havdalah - Prayer recited at the conclusion of Shabbos and Yom Tov to divide between a holy day and a weekday.

Hechsher - Rabbinical supervision.

Hefker - Ownerless.

Kabbalah - Jewish mysticism.

Kebeitza - A volume measure (approx. 60 cc).

Kezayis (pl. *kezaysim*) - A volume measure (approx. 30 cc).

Kiddush - Sanctification of Shabbos and Yom Tov, usually recited over a cup of wine.

Kitniyos - Foods not eaten by Ashkenazim during Pesach.

Kittel - White outer garment.

Kneidlach - Boiled matza-meal balls.

Korban Pesach - Pesach Sacrifice.

Lechem Mishneh - Two complete loaves used on Shabbos and Yom Tov as a commemoration of the double portion of manna that fell on *erev Shabbos* and *erev Yom Tov*.

Lulav - Palm branch, one of the four species taken on Succos.

Ma'ariv - The evening prayer.

Mayim acharonim - Washing hands before *bensching*.

Midrash - Commentary on the Bible.

Mikveh - Ritual immersion pool.

Mincha - The afternoon prayer.

Mincha Gedola - The earliest time when the *Mincha* prayer may be recited.

Minyan - Quorum of men required for communal prayer.

Mishnah - The basis of the Oral Law.

Mitzrayim - Egypt.

Mitzvah (pl. Mitzvos) - A commandment.

Mashiach - The Messiah.

Motzai Shabbos - The night after Shabbos.

Nach - The books of the Bible, excluding *chumash*.

Pidyon Haben - Redemption of the firstborn.

Rabban - Senior Rabbi.

Rav (pl. Rabbonim) - Rabbi.

Retzei - Paragraph added to bensching on Shabbos.

Reviyis - Liquid measure (approx. 86cc or. 3 fl. oz.).

Seuda Shelishis - Third meal that is eaten on Shabbos.

Seudas Mitzvah - Meal eaten to celebrate a mitzvah, e.g. wedding, circumcision, redemption of the firstborn etc.

Shacharis - The morning service.

Shechina - The Divine presence.

Shehakol - B'racha recited for certain foods.

Shehecheyanu - Blessing of thanks recited on joyous occasions.

Shemos - The book of Exodus.

Shir Hashirim - The Song of Songs.

Shiur (pl. *shiurim*) - A lesson in the Torah.

Shemittah - The final year of the seven year agricultural cycle.

Shulchan Aruch - Code of Jewish law.

Siyum - Festive meal made at the conclusion of a tractate, etc.

Tamei - Unclean, physically or spiritually.

Tanach - The Bible.

Tehillim - The book of Psalms.

Tzaddik (pl. *Tzaddikim*) - Righteous individual.

Vilna Gaon - Rabbi Eliahu (1720-1797), Genius of Vilna and leader of Eastern European Jewry.

Yaakov Avinu - Jacob the Patriarch.

Ya'aleh Ve'yavo - Additional prayer recited on Yom Tov and *Rosh Chodesh*.

Yechezkel - The book of Ezekiel.

Yetzias Mitzrayim - The Exodus from Egypt.

Yitzchak Avinu - Isaac the Patriarch.

Yoel - The book of Joel.

Yom Tov - Jewish holiday.

Zimun - Invitation to bensch, made in the presence of at least three men.

מקורות

פרק א - בדיקת חמץ

[1] סימן תלא סעיף א. [2] פשוט ועיין סי' תלה ומ"ב סק"ב. [3] מ"ב סק"ח. [4] מ"ב שם, הליכות שלמה פ"ב הערה 62, אג"מ ח"ד סי' צט. [5] מ"ב סק"א. [6] מבית לוי מועדי השנה עמוד רכט אות ט. [7] סימן תלו סעיף א מ"ב סק"ג, מנחת יצחק ח"ח סי' לה. [8] מבית לוי מועדי השנה עמוד רלג אות טו. [9] סימן תלו סעיף א, שערי ימי הפסח עמוד לג אות ט. [10] שו"ת שבט הלוי ח"ד סי' מד, תשובות והנהגות ח"ב סי' ריא (ג), ועיין הליכות שלמה (פסח) פ"ה סעיף יח. [11] שם. [12] מבית לוי מועדי השנה עמוד רלב סעיף יד, סידור פסח כהלכתו פי"ב סעיף ט. [13] סימן תלא סעיף ב מ"ב סק"ה, יב. [14] מ"ב סק"ז ושעה"צ סק"ז. [15] סעיף ג ומ"ב סק"ו. [16] מ"ב סי' תרעא סק"י, סי' רלה ס"ק יז. [17] הלכה של פסח ח"א עמוד סא סעיף לב. [18] סימן תלב סעיף ב ושעה"צ ס"ק יב. [19] שע"ת סי' תלב סק"ג. [20] חוט שני עמוד סב ד"ה ואם, שערי ימי הפסח עמוד לט סעיף ה. [21] הליכות שלמה פסח פ"ה סעיף א, סי' תלד מ"ב סק"א. [22] סימן תלא סעיף א, סי' תלד סעיף ג, מ"ב ס"ק יט, כה"ח סק"ל. [23] מ"ב סי' תלו ס"ק לב. [24] חוט שני עמוד נט, מבית לוי מועדי השנה עמוד רכח אות ד, הליכות שלמה פסח פ"ה סעיף יא, הגדת הגריש"א עמוד 17. [25] שם. [26] הליכות שלמה פסח פרק ה ס"ק יט, חוט שני שם. [27] סי' תלב סעיף א. [28] מ"ב סק"ד. [29] מ"ב סק"ח. [30] סעיף ב מ"ב סק"ט. [31] מ"ב סק"י, ח. [32] סעיף א ומ"ב סק"ה. [33] מ"ב סק"ו, סעיף א. [34] סעיף ב. [35] כה"ח ס"ק כב. [36] פשוט. [37] הלכה של פסח ח"א עמוד עה סעיף ג. [38] פשוט.

פרק ב - תענית בכורות

[39] סימן תע סעיף א-ב. [40] סימן תקסד. [41] מ"ב סי' תע סק"ב, ד. [42] מבית לוי מועדי השנה עמוד רעו סעיף ג. [43] חק יעקב סק"ב, כה"ח סק"ח. [44] רמ"א סעיף ב מ"ב סק"ט-י, ערוה"ש סעיף ב. [45] מ"ב סק"י. [46] סידור פסח כהלכתו פי"ד הערה 14, מנחת יצחק ח"ט סי' מה, תשובות והנהגות ח"ב סי' רי. [47] מבית לוי מועדי השנה עמוד רעח סעיף ח. [48] מנחת יצחק שם, סידור פסח כהלכתו פי"ד

סעיף 13*. [49] סידור פסח כהלכתו פי"ד סעיף ו, אגרות משה ח"א סי' נקז, שו"ת משנה הלכות ח"ו סימן קסו. [50] מנחת יצחק ח"ד סי' צג. [51] סידור פסח כהלכתו פי"ד סעיף ח. [52] שו"ת בצל החכמה ח"ד סי' ק. [53] מ"ב סק"ב. [54] מבית לוי מועדי השנה עמוד רעח סעיף ט.

פרק ג - ערב פסח

[55] מ"ב סימן תכט ס"ק יג. [56] סימן תמג סעיף א, מ"ב סק"ח, מבית לוי מועדי השנה עמוד רפב סעיף יד. [57] רמ"א סימן תמה סעיף א, מ"ב תלג ס"ק כח. [58] סידור פסח כהלכתו פט"ו סעיף ד ע"פ רמ"א ריש סימן תמה. [59] פשוט. [60] מ"ב סי' תמה סק"ז. [61] מ"ב סי' תמה סק"א. [62] מ"ב סי' תמה סק"א. [63] מ"ב סק"ז. [64] מ"ב סק"ה. [65] מ"ב סי' תלג ס"ק מז. [66] מ"ב סימן תלד ס"ק יא, דעת תורה סוף סעיף ג. [67] סי' תלד מ"ב ס"ק יב. [68] הלכות חג בחג פ"ח הלכה יד. [69] סימן תסח סעיף א מ"ב סק"ז. [70] מ"ב סק"ז. [71] שם. [72] מ"ב סק"ז. [73] ארחות רבינו ח"ב עמוד נו. [74] מבית לוי מועדי השנה עמוד רפא סעיף יג. [75] שם. [76] רמ"א סי' תסח סעיף ב, ומ"ב סק"ח. [77] רמ"א סי' תעא סעיף ב. [78] הגדת הגריש"א עמוד 18, שערי ימי הפסח עמוד כד סעיף ב. [79] רמ"א שם, ומ"ב ס"ק יג. [80] סידור פסח כהלכתו פט"ו סעיף יד, שבט הלוי ח"ח סי' קיז אות ה. [81] מ"ב סי' תעא סק"כ, חיי אדם כלל קכט סימן יג. [82] חק יעקב סימן תעא סק"כ, סידור פסח כהלכתו פט"ז הערה 42*. [83] סימן תעא סעיף א, מ"ב סק"ג. [84] לוח א"י, מעשה רב אות קצ. [85] מ"ב סי' תעא ס"ק כב. [86] מ"ב סי' קכח ס"ק קסה, מ"ב סי' תעא סק"כ, חיי אדם כלל עט סימן קא. [87] מ"ב שם, כה"ח סי' תסח ס"ק קא.

פרק ד - עירוב תבשילין

[88] סי' תקכז סעיף א. [89] שם. [90] פשוט. [91] סעיף ז, שעה"צ סק"מ, מ"ב ס"ק נו. [92] בסעיף יט מובא ב' שיטות לענין הדלקת הנר, מ"ב ס"ק נה, כה"ח ס"ק קיג, שש"כ פמ"ד סעיף יב. וכ"כ בשו"ת באר משה ח"ז עמוד שז אות ד, ספר עירוב תבשילין הערוך עמוד

פ בשם החזו"א, ובמנחת יצחק ח"ט סי' נד (ג). [93] סעיף ז, מנחת יצחק ח"ז סי' לו. [94] עיין אשל אברהם מבוטשאטש ריש הסימן, ומחה"ש ס"ק י"א, ועיין מש"כ הגרש"א הובא מבקשי תורה יו"ט עמוד ריח שבניו הנשואים שאוכלים אצל אביהם כל ימי החג והשבת א"צ לעשות עירוב תבשילין, ועיין מנחת יצחק ח"ט סי' נז (ג). [95] מ"ב סי' תצו ס"ק יג. [96] פשוט. [97] ביה"ל סעיף א ד"ה ספק חשיכה, מבקשי תורה סי' מט פ"ג עמוד רטז בשם הגריש"א, ערוה"ש סעיף יד, שו"ת שבט הלוי ח"ט סי' קכט (ד). [98] ערוך השלחן סעיף יד. [99] מ"ב סק"ד, ביה"ל סי' רסא ד"ה ומערבין. [100] סעיף ב, מ"ב סק"ה, ו, יא, סעיף ה, מ"ב ס"ק יג. [101] מ"ב סק"ח, לקט הלכות יו"ט פי"ט סעיף ד, בן איש חי שנה א' פרשת צו אות א. [102] שבט הלוי ח"ט סי' קכט. [103] סעיף ג. [104] סעיף ד ומ"ב ס"ק יב. [105] ביה"ל סעיף ו ד"ה עדשים. [106] סעיף טו, טז. [107] מ"ב ס"ק מח, יא, ששכ פ"ב הערה לז. [108] סעיף ז ומ"ב ס"ק כד. [109] מ"ב סק"ג, ביה"ל ד"ה וע"י עירובי וכו'. [110] סעיף יג, מ"ב ס"ק מא.

פרק ה - הדלקת נרות יום טוב

[111] פרמ"ג סי' תקיד מש"ז ס"ק יב, מבית לוי מועדי השנה עמוד תמד סעיף א. [112] פשוט. [113] סי' רצט סעיף י ומ"ב ס"ק לו, וסי' תקיד ס"ק לה. [114] סי' רסא מ"ב סק"ב, ששכ סעיף יז. [115] חיי אדם כלל צב סי' ב. [116] מבקשי תורה סי' מט עמוד רלא בשם הגרש"א והגריש"א, ובלקט הלכות יו"ט שם סעיף ו בשם הגר"ש ואזנר והגרנ"ק, ואיסור עשיית חור גם. [117] מבקשי תורה סי' ד ענף ב סעיף ו בשם הגרשז"א ולקט הלכות יו"ט פי"ד סעיף ח. [118] סי' תקיד סעיף ט, ששכ פל"ה סעיף כ. [119] מ"ב סי' תקא ס"ק לד. [120] הקדמת בן הפרישה ליו"ד בשם אמו, ששכ פמ"ד סעיף ב. [121] וביו"ט עצמו אסור להדליק קודם צאה"כ משום איסור הכנה כמבואר בסי' תקיד שם ובמטה אפרים סי' תקצקט סעיף י. [122] פשוט. [123] סי' רצט סעיף ו ומ"ב ס"ק לו. [124] בן הפרישה בהקדמה ליו"ד בשם אמו, מ"ב סי' רסג ס"ק כו. מג"א סי' רסג ס"ק יב, גר"ז סעיף ח שלא לשנות שאין לנשים שכל לחלק בין המקרים. מטה אפרים סי' לג הובא בהליכות בת ישראל פי"ד סעיף ז, ששכ פמ"ד סעיף ז. [125] ששכ פמ"ד סעיף ז. [126] פשוט. [127] ריש סי' תקב, ביה"ל סי' תקיא סעיף ד ד"ה אין עושין מוגמר וכו', ששכ פי"ג סעיף ח ופמ"ד סעיף ט. [128] ריש סי' תקב, מ"ב סי' תרעא סק"א, הליכות בת ישראל

פט"ו סעיף נג, שם סעיף נב, ספר זכור ושמור הל' יו"ט ח"ג G1(d), ביה"ל סי' תקיא סעיף ד ד"ה אין עושין מוגמר וכו', ששכ פי"ג סעיף ח ופמ"ד סעיף ט. [129] אג"מ או"ח ח"ד סי' קא (א), מנחת שלמה ח"ב סי' נח (ב) [אמנם, הגרש"ז הורה בביתו לא לענות אמן]. ועיין בשבט הלוי ח"ג סי' סט שכתב שבפסח וסוכות צריכה לענות אמן, שמסתמא לא כללה שאר מצוות החג (סוכה, אכילת מצה וכו') כשהיא ברכה שהחיינו בהדלקת נרות, והבעל מוציאה בשהחיינו שהוא מברך על שאר מצוות הלילה. וע"ע בשש"כ פמ"ג סעיף ד. [130] כן שמענו בשם הגר"צ ובר. [131] סי' תצ סעיף ז מ"ב ס"ק יג. [132] מבית לוי מועדי השנה עמוד תמו סעיף ח.

פרק ו - הכנות לסדר

[133] פסחים קיז סוף עמוד ב, רשב"ם צט עמוד ב ד"ה ולא יפחתו לו. [134] סי' תעב סעיף יא, מ"ב ס"ק לח. [135] מבית לוי מועדי השנה עמוד רפח סעיף א, מ"ב סי' שכ ס"ק נו. [136] מבית לוי מועדי השנה עמוד רפח סעיף ב. [137] סעיף י, מ"ב ס"ק לה, לז, כה"ח ס"ק עב. [138] הגדה קול דודי פ"ג אות ד בשם הגרמ"פ, הלילה הזה עמוד 11 בשם הגריש"א. [139] מ"ב סי' קעה סק"ב, הסדר הערוך פי"ד אות יד. [140] מ"ב ס"ק לז, הלכה של פסח ח"ב עמוד קפה. [141] ביה"ל סי' רעא סעיף יג ד"ה של רביעית. [142] מ"ב סק"ל. [143] פסקי תשובות סי' תעב אות ז. [144] רמ"א סי' תעג סעיף א, הלכה של פסח ח"ב עמוד קצא סעיף לה. [145] שמות פרק יב פסוק יז, סימן תנג סעיף ד. [146] מ"ב סי' תנג ס"ק כא. [147] הלכה של פסח ח"א עמוד תפא. [148] ביה"ל ריש סימן תס. [149] מ"ב סי' תס סק"ב, ערוה"ש סק"ז, סי' תנג סעיף ד. [150] רמב"ם חו"מ פ"א ה"א, שיעורי תורה סי' ג סעיף יב, שיעורין של תורה שיעורי המצות אות כד. [151] מ"ב סימן תפו סק"א. [152] סי' תעה סעיף א, מ"ב ס"ק טז, סימן תעז סעיף ו ומ"ב סק"א, סי' תפו סעיף א ומ"ב סק"א. [153] פשוט. [154] כנ"ל. [155] מנחת חינוך מצוה ו, מצוה י, מצות מצה פי"ג בכ"ג. [156] פשוט. [157] פשוט. [158] סי' שו סעיף ס"ג, ששכ פכ"ט סעיף מ. [159] מ"ב ס"ק טו, צי"א חי"ג סי' טו אות ח-ט. [160] מ"ב ס"ק לד, כה"ח ס"ק עב, חיי"א כלל קל סק"ג. [161] מ"ב ס"ק מב. [162] כך יצא ע"י מדידות מדויקות, סדר פסח כהלכתו ח"ב פרק ט סעיף יא. [163] מ"ב ס"ק לח. [164] מ"ב ס"ק לו, סדר פסח כהלכתו ח"ב פ"ט סעיף ד. [165] סימן תעג סעיף כ, ערוה"ש סעיף יא. [166] חק יעקב

סימן תעה אות ו. [167] כה"ח ס"ק נח. [168] רמ"א ס"ו ס תעה. [169] באר היטב סק"ח, ערוה"ש סעיף יא. [170] פשוט, ועיין כה"ח הנ"ל שכן צריך לעשות לכתחילה. [171] מ"ב ס"ק יז. [172] באר היטב סק"ח, חיי אדם כלל קל הסדר בקצרה ס"ק יא. [173] כה"ח ס' תעג סק"ס, וע' סדר הערוך פי"ט ס"ע' ד שהמקור לקחת צואר העוף מרש"י בס' האורה שכ' שהיו נתפחים מפרקותיהם של ישראל מהחומר הכבד שעל כתפיהם, פרמ"ג א"א סק"ז. [174] מ"ב ס"ק לב. [175] סעיף ד וברמ"א, מ"ב ס"ק לב. [176] ויגד משה סימן ג אות י. [177] מ"ב ס"ק יא, סי' תעג ס"ק יא. [178] רמ"א סי' תעג סעיף ה. [179] קיצור שו"ע סי' קיח סעיף ב, ערוה"ש סי' תעג סק"י. [180] רמב"ם חו"מ פרק ז הלכה ו-ז. [181] רמ"א סי' תעב סעיף ד, מועדים וזמנים ח"ג סי' רנז. [182] מוע"ז שם, שמע בני עמוד 63 בשם הגרחפ"ש. [183] מ"ב ס' תעב ס"ק יג. [184] מ"ב סק"ז, ומש"כ תחת ראשו אמר הגרח"ק שלא נהגו כן. [185] מ"ב סק"ח. [186] מ"ב ס"ק ט. [187] סעיף ג, מ"ב סק"ט. [188] רמ"א סעיף ג, מ"ב ס"ק יא. [189] סימן תעב סעיף ז, סימן תעז סעיף א. [190] רמ"א סימן תעב סעיף ז. [191] מ"ב ס' תעג ס"ק עא. [192] סימן תעו סעיף א. [193] מ"ב סק"א. [194] שם. [195] ויגד משה סימן יב ד"ה ואולי. [196] מ"ב סי' תעב ס"ק יג, וע"ע הליכות שלמה פסח פ"ט הערה 136. [197] פסקי תשובות בשם גריש"א הערה 14. [198] תעב סע' ב, מ"ב סק"ו, הסדר הערוך פי"ג ס"ע' ז, וע' תרגום יונתן בן עוזיאל בראשית פכ"ז פ"א, ובעל הטורים שם פסוק כז. [199] פשוט. [200] ערוה"ש סי' קפב סעיף א. [201] הלכה של פסח ח"ב עמוד שפח סעיף לח. [202] גר"ז סימן תעב ס"ק לא. [203] פשוט. [204] סימן תקכז.

פרק ז - פסח שחל במוצאי שבת

[205] ס' תע סע' ב. [206] ס' תמד סע' א, מ"ב סק"א. [207] פסקי תשובות סימן תמד אות יז. [208] סע' ב, מ"ב סק"ט, י. [209] ביה"ל סע' א. [210] שע"ת סוף הסימן. [211] מ"ב ס' תעג סק"ל, ס' תקד ס"ק יט. [212] מבית לוי מועדי השנה עמוד שיז, מ"ב ס' תמד ס"ק כא, שש"כ פי"ל הע' קכא. [213] ע' אג"מ ח"א ס' קנה ד"ה ולכן טוב שהתיר. ומבית לוי מועדי השנה עמוד שכא אסר. ולמעשה אינו נוגע כ"כ שבזה"ז קשה להשיג מצה עשירה עם השגחה מעולה. [214] רמ"א ס' תעא סע' ב ומ"ב ס"ק יד, מג"א סק"ו, ס' רצא הנ"ל ד"ה נמצא שלמעשה. [215] מ"ב ס' תמד סק"ח, וס' רצא ס"ק טו, אגרות חזו"א

ח"א ס' קפח. [216] מ"ב ס"ק כב. [217] מ"ב ס' רצ סק"ד. [218] רמ"א ס' תמד סע' א, מ"ב סק"ח. [219] מ"ב ס' רצט ס"ק לו.

פרק ח - הסדר

[220] מהרי"ל ריש הלכות סדר ההגדה. [221] יסוד ושורש העבודה שער ט, ריש פ"ו. [222] שם. [223] רמב"ם חו"מ פרק ו ה"א, פרק ז ה"א. [224] שם פרק ז הל' ז, י, יב. [225] ס' תעג סע' ד. [226] רמ"א שם, סימן תעב סעיף א. [227] ס' תעב סע' יד, מ"ב ס"ק מד. [228] סימן תעב סעיף טו מ"ב ס"ק מז, הלכה של פסח ח"ב עמוד קצז סעיף נב. [229] חינוך בהלכה עמוד 181. [230] הלכה של פסח ח"ב עמוד רלז סעיף מג. [231] מ"ב ס' תעב סק"ג. [232] ויגד משה סימן ט אות ז, תרגום יונתן בן עוזיאל בראשית כז:א. [233] רמ"א ס"ו סק"נ, מ"ב ס"ק עח. [234] ויגד משה סימן טו אות ו-ז, סדר פסח כהלכתו ח"ב פ"ג סעיף ו. [235] שש"כ פרק מ"ז הערה כו. [236] מ"ב ס' תעג ס"ק טז, גר"ז ס"ק יג, מ"ב ס' ר"ח ס"ק עב ושעה"צ ס"ק עא, ולענין שאר משקין, יש חשש מוסיף על הכוסות אם מברך שהכל. [237] מבית לוי מועדי השנה עמוד רצז, סדר פסח כהלכתו ח"ב פרק ג סעיף ו. [238] שם, שמענו מאת הגר"ז ובר. [239] מ"ב ס' תעב סק"ל. [240] מחצית השקל סק"א בשם הב"ח, שעה"צ סי' רי ס"ק יא, מ"ב ס' תעב ס"ק לד. [241] סימן תעג סעיף א, מ"ב סק"ג, הלכה של פסח ח"ב עמוד צו-צח. [242] מ"ב ס' תעב ס"ק כא. [243] הלילה הזה עמוד 13 בשם גריש"א. [244] מ"ב ס' תעג סק"א. [245] הלכה של פסח ח"ב עמוד רפז סעיף כג. [246] שם סעיף כו. [247] מ"ב ס' תעב ס"ק כא. [248] סימן תעג סעיף ו, שעה"צ ס"ק סט, ט"ז סק"ו, מ"ב ס' קנח סק"כ. [249] סדר פסח כהלכתו ח"ב פ"ד סעיף א והערה 2, מבית לוי עמוד רצז, ויגד משה פט"ו סעיף ה. [250] מ"ב ס' קנח סק"כ, וע"ע הליכות שלמה פ"ט ס"ק נג. [251] סדר פסח כהלכתו שם. [252] שם סעיף ג. [253] מ"ב ס' תעג ס"ק יט, כא. [254] מ"ב ס"ק כא, ב"ח ד"ה ולוקח, רבינו מנוח על הרמב"ם פ"ח ה"ב. [255] מבית לוי עמוד רצט. [256] סימן תעג סעיף ו. [257] מ"ב ס' קנה ס"ק כו, חג בחג עמוד תקכה. [258] מבית לוי שם. [259] כה"ח ס"ק נב. [260] מ"ב ס' תעג ס"ק נז. [261] מ"ב ס"ק נח, חק יעקב סימן תעה ס"ק כו. [262] הסדר הערוך פנ"ז סעיף ז. [263] חיי אדם כלל הסדר בקצרה סס"ג. [264] ספר המצוות לרמב"ם מ"ע קנז. [265] רמ"א סי' תעג סעיף ו, מ"ב ס"ק סג, סד. [266] מ"ב שם. [267] ע' מ"ב שם שכתב תכנס שאשה תכנס ותשמע

וכו', וע' מעשה רב אות קצא שכ' "ואומר הגדה וכולם שומעים". [268]
כה"ח ס"ק קכו, מ"ב סק"ס. [269] סעיף ו, מ"ב ס"ק סו. [270] סעיף
ז. [271] ביה"ד ד"ה הרשות בידו, הליכות שלמה פ"ט סעיף לד, הגדת
הגריש"א עמוד 24. [272] סעיף ז. [273] מ"ב סק"ע. [274] הלכה של
פסח ח"ב עמוד קסו סעיף ז. [275] סימן תעז סעיף א. [276] חג בחג
עמוד תקלז ע"פ אור החיים במדבר פ"ט פי"ד. [277] מ"ב ס' תעג ס"ק
עא. [278] רמ"א סו"ס תעג. [279] מ"ב ס"ק עד, שעה"צ ס"ק פא, ועיין
דרכי משה אות יח. [280] מהרי"ל סדר הגדה אות כז, כה"ח ס"ק קסח.
[281] ויגד משה פכ"ג סעיף יא. [282] קול דודי פי"א סעיף יב. [283]
סימן תעה סעיף א. [284] שם. [285] ביה"ד ד"ה יטול ידיו. [286] מ"ב
ס"ק כד. [287] פשוט. [288] מ"ב ס' תפו סק"א, הלכה של פסח ח"ב
עמוד קנו סעיף סב. [289] חינוך בהלכה עמוד 181. [290] ויגד משה
פכ"ד סעיף ח. [291] שם פכ"ג סעיף ג. [292] חג בחג עמוד תקמז.
[293] שם. [294] שם. [295] פרי מגדים משב"ז סימן תפו. [296] סימן
תעה סעיף א. [297] קול דודי פי"ג סעיף א. [298] סעיף א. [299]
פשוט. [300] סעיף א מ"ב סק"ב. [301] שם. [302] מ"ב סק"ט, הלכה
של פסח ח"ב עמוד קנב. [303] הגדת גריש"א עמוד 25. [304] מ"ב
סק"ד. [305] שיעורין של תורה, שיעורי המצוות אות ל, חג בחג עמוד
תקנ. [306] הלילה הזה עמוד 19 ע"פ מ"ב סימן תסא ס"ק יח. [307]
מ"ב סימן תעב ס"ק כב. [308] מ"ב ס' תעה ס"ק לד. [309] כך יצא
ע"י מדידות מדויקות. [310] סדר פסח כהלכתו פ"ט סעיף יא. [311]
מ"ב ס' תעג סק"מ, ויגד משה פכ"א סעיף ג. [312] הלילה הזה עמוד
20. [313] מ"ב ס' תעה ס"ק יג, רמ"א סימן תעג סעיף ה. [314] תוס'
פסחים דף קטז עמוד א ד"ה צריך, קול דודי פט"ו סעיף כג. [315]
מ"ב ס' תעה ס"ק יג. [316] רמ"א ס' ריג סעיף א, מ"ב ס"ק יב. [317]
הלכה של פסח ח"ב עמוד רלד סעיף כה. [318] גר"ז סימן תעה ס"ק
כט. [319] מ"ב ס"ק יד. [320] תפארת ישראל פסחים פ"י אות טו.
[321] מ"ב ס' תעה ס"ק טז. [322] סעיף א, סדר פסח כהלכתו ח"ב
פ"ח סעיף יד. [323] עיין מ"ב סימן תפו סק"א. [324] מ"ב ס"ק טז.
[325] מ"ב ס"ק יט. [326] קיצור שו"ע סימן קיט סעיף ז, ערוה"ש סימן
תעה סעיף ז. [327] סעיף א, ביה"ל ד"ה ואומר, קיצור שו"ע סימן קיט
סעיף ז, גר"ז ס"ק יח. [328] הלילה הזה עמוד 21. [329] סעיף א, מ"ב
ס"ק כג. [330] גר"ז סק"כ. [331] רמ"א ס' תעו סעיף ב, מ"ב ס"ק יא,
ויגד משה פכ"ז סעיף ה, מבית לוי עמוד שח. [332] סדר הערוך פצ"ד

סעיף יב. [333] סימן תעו סעיף א, מ"ב סק"א, סימן תעג ס"ק לב.
[334] רמ"א סימן תעו סעיף ב. [335] סימן תעז סעיף א. [336] הלכה
של פסח ח"ב עמוד שנג סעיף יט, הליכות שלמה סוף פרק ט. [337]
רמ"א סימן תעב סעיף ז, ויגד משה פכ"ז סעיף יד. [338] ויגד משה
פכ"ז סעיף יג ד"ה והנה ע"ש סימן תקכקד סעיף א. [339] ימי
הפסח עמוד קנד בשם גרנ"ק. [340] פסחים דף קיט/ב. [341] הגדת
אליהו כי טוב עמוד ריב. [342] סימן תעז סעיף א. [343] שם. [344]
הלכה של פסח ח"ב עמוד ש סעיף לט. [345] רמ"א סו"ס ב. [346]
מ"ב סק"א, חג בחג עמוד שיז. [347] מ"ב שם. [348] מ"ב סימן תעה
ס"ק לד, מצות השם סדר אכילת הפסח. [349] סימן תעז סעיף א.
[350] מ"ב סק"ד, וסימן תעב ס"ק כג, אגרות משה ח"ג סימן סז. [351]
סעיף א, מ"ב סק"ו. [352] סעיף ב, מ"ב ס"ק ט, יא, טז, יז. [353] סימן
תעה סעיף א, מ"ב סק"א. [354] מ"ב שם. [355] מ"ב סק"ב, סימן תפא
סק"א, רמ"א סו"ס קצז, הלילה הזה עמוד 22. [356] סימן תעט סעיף א
מ"ב סק"א. [357] סדר הערוך פ"ר סע' כ בשם לקט יושר עמ' לו ד"ה
וזכרוני, שבעל תרה"ד נטל מי"א רק בליל הסדר. [358] רמ"א סו"ס
תעט, מ"ב ס"ק יג. [359] מ"ב סימן ס סק"י. [360] ויגד משה פכ"ט
סעיף ה, קול דודי פי"ט סעיף ו. [361] כה"ח סימן קפג ס"ק יט, קצות
השלחן סימן מו ס"ק כא. [362] סימן קפח סעיף ו. [363] תשובות
והנהגות ח"א סימן שח. [364] ויגד משה פ"ל סעיף ג, ו. [365] שם
סעיף ד. [366] שם סעיף ה. [367] רמ"א סו"ס תפ. [368] שם. [369]
ערוה"ש ס' תעף סעיף יד. [370] מ"ב סימן ס סק"י. [371] סימן תעב סעיף יד.
[372] גר"ז ס"ק כה. [373] ויגד משה פל"א סעיף ד ע"פ רש"י פסחים
דף לו עמוד א ד"ה שעונין עליו דברים. [374] ויגד משה שם סעיף ח,
קול דודי פ"כ סעיף ד. [375] באר היטב סו"ס תעג. [376] ויגד משה
פל"א סעיף ב. [377] מ"ב סימן תפ סק"ה. [378] שם. [379] מ"ב
סימן תעב סק"ל, סימן תעד סק"ג. [380] חג בחג עמוד תקכא. [381]
שם. [382] מ"ב סימן רח ס"ק נח. [383] חיי אדם הסדר בקצרה סעיף
טז. [384] שיר השירים רבה פרק א סימן יא. [385] סימן תפא סעיף
ב, חג בחג עמוד תקסז. [386] רמ"א סו"ס תפא, מ"ב סק"ד. [387]
פרי מגדים א"א ריש סימן תמד, מ"ב סימן רצט ס"ק לו. [388] פשוט.
[389] יו"ט שני כהלכתו פ"א הערה קצח בשם הגרשז"א. [390] ויגד
משה פכ"ח סעיף יא. [391] באר היטב סימן תפא סק"ג. [392] ויגד
משה פל"ג סעיף ב.

Kezayis of Lettuce for Maror
Actual size